Chris Barber has spent most of his life in south Wales where he has been able to pursue his fascination for exploring wild and remote places. Currently a local government officer with special responsibility for Gwent's Countryside Warden Service, he has also worked as an industrial technician and as an instructor at an outdoor activity centre. A skilled photographer, he also pursues an active interest in hill walking, caving and mountaineering. He has written several books on Wales, including *Exploring the Brecon Beacons National Park*, *Ghosts of Wales* and *Mysterious Wales*.

CHRIS BARBER

More Mysterious Wales

PALADIN
GRAFTON BOOKS
A Division of the Collins Publishing Group

LONDON GLASGOW
TORONTO SYDNEY AUCKLAND

Paladin
Grafton Books
A Division of the Collins Publishing Group
8 Grafton Street, London W1X 3LA

Published in Paladin 1987

First published in Great Britain by
David & Charles Publishers 1986

All photographs are by the author, except for
those on pages 174 by Dr Hugh Parry and
page 215 by John Idris Jones

ISBN 0-586-08518-1

Printed in Great Britain by
St Edmundsbury Press, Bury St Edmunds, Suffolk

Set in Baskerville

'*Myths and legends have hidden meanings. We are becomingly increasingly aware that they are like cryptograms waiting to be decoded. In spite of everything they remain a fragile link between us and a remote past.*'

The Mysteries of Stonehenge
Fernand Niel

Contents

Introduction

*'Legend is history, in the sense that the legends and
traditions of a people are part of its history.'*

G. H. Doble, *Lives of The Welsh Saints*

When I completed *Mysterious Wales* in 1982 I found that I had so
much material left over and had identified so many more paths to
follow that it seemed a good idea to write a second volume, dealing
with more obscure locations and giving a special emphasis to the
mysteries of the Dark Ages, which I find particularly fascinating.

During my research, I came to see the map of Wales as a giant
jigsaw puzzle with names of villages, churches, and geographical
features such as hills, rivers, valleys and woods linking with a
complex web of folklore, stories of Celtic saints, church foundations,
ancient kingdoms and memories of battles. A great deal of my
research and associated wanderings have been associated with
locations and events tied in with the fifth and sixth centuries. This
was the golden age of the Celtic saints; the time of Arthur and
Maelgwyn Gwynedd, a period of Welsh history that is post-Roman
and pre-Norman. It is fascinating that so many place names and
features of the landscape can be linked with a period of history that
is so shrouded in mystery.

Researching the two books was a very enjoyable experience,
providing a reason to wander around odd corners of Wales, visiting
places that I would otherwise probably never have seen. On some
occasions I arrived in a hamlet armed with some long-forgotten
information, which I had gathered through hours of patient
research, and to my delight was able to bring to people's notice
certain relics in their neighbourhood that had become forgotten
and were now ignored.

I have endeavoured to include a wide variety of ancient sites
with an associated mixture of folklore and history and have set out
to show the various connections between different sites (such as
interrelating inscribed stones) where possible.

Following the publication of *Mysterious Wales*, I received many
interesting letters, but I was particularly intrigued one evening

North Escarpment, Black Mountains, Powys

when I had a telephone call from a Cardiff man who told me that he and his colleague had identified King Arthur and discovered the location of his grave. He realized that I would be interested in the project and, as a photographer, I was invited to take a series of photographs for a book that they were currently writing on their discoveries. In due course, I heard the full account of their amazing story. To my mind it is the best Arthurian theory that has ever been produced. With their permission I have included a brief outline of their claims and discoveries, which deserve to be taken seriously.

The reader will find that a large proportion of this book is linked with the Arthurian period. In particular, it shows the importance of inscribed memorial stones relating to the people of those times, and includes the exciting recent discovery of a sixth-century stone which, it is claimed, bears an inscription relating to King Arthur and his father.

I have tried to demonstrate that legends are mostly based on historical happenings and connected incidents. This book contains a mass of information, but it is only intended as a brief introduction to a variety of intriguing places in Wales. There is no substitute for further research and enquiry by the reader.

Chris Barber
Llanfoist, Abergavenny

MAPS

Wales is covered by 23 maps in the Ordnance Survey series 1:50,000. For greater detail 1:25,000 (2½in to the mile) maps may be used, but six times the number would be required to cover the same area, which would prove expensive for the casual visitor.

GRID REFERENCES

The locations of the sites are given whenever possible as six figure grid references: for example, SJ 172679 (116). The relevant Ordnance Survey 1:50,000 map number is given in brackets after the grid reference to enable the reader to identify the appropriate map easily.

SPELLING OF PLACE NAMES

Generally, the Ordnance Survey spelling of place names has been used to assist the reader with identification of sites on the map.

ACKNOWLEDGEMENTS

I am most grateful to the numerous friends and people whom I met on my travels around Wales and who helped me in a variety of ways. Thanks are also due to Alan Wilson and Mick Blackett for giving me permission to include extracts from their work on the discovery of King Arthur.

1.
Prehistoric
Stone
Enigmas

'Hoary and lichened by age, grim
and fretted by a thousand storms
Our ancient megalithic monuments
are still numerous, massive and
full of mystery.'

Walter Johnson
Folk-Memory

Standing stones are to be found throughout Britain as well as in many other parts of the world. In Wales they are known as maenhirs (longstones) and are generally erected as single stones, unhewn and mysteriously pointing towards the sky or leaning at an angle, either by design or perhaps through vandalism or subsidence.

Many suggestions have been made to explain their purpose. Were they erected as markers on ancient trackways? Or were they perhaps put up as monuments to commemorate persons of importance? The maenhir is certainly the forerunner of the Christian memorial stone and many of them were converted into inscribed stones and pillar crosses.

Excavations have failed, in many cases, to reveal any trace of interments beneath the stones, so as many of them do not mark actual graves perhaps their erection was symbolic. In many instances, they seem to be placed close to burial mounds and it is feasible that they were intended as markers to indicate a monumental mound.

Over the years, the stones have become objects of superstition and many strange legends have become associated with them. Some of the stones are supposed to walk, dance and roam around in the night, visiting local pools or rivers for a drink or a swim. It was once said that anyone who planned to visit the site of a 'wandering megalith' during its absence, to seek treasure at its base, would not live to see the morning. The tradition that stones and burial chambers conceal treasure is common to many of these sites, and there are numerous tales told of farmers harnessing teams of oxen to stones in order to uproot them. But they never seem to succeed, for the stones are always set too deep in the ground or else the men are frightened away by lightning, thunder and torrential rain.

Many of the standing stones and cromlechs around Wales are supposed to have been thrown to their sites by giants, by King Arthur or by Merlin the magician. The giant Idris Gawr, for example, is reputed to have thrown Llech Idris a 10 foot stone (near Trawsfynydd) from the summit of Cader Idris. On another occasion he threw a stone known as Y Garreg Ddu from Carn Fadrun to Rhiw Mountain on the Lleyn peninsula. Carreg Samson

Standing stone near Llanrhaeadr-ym-mochnant, Powys

near Aberdaron in Dyfed was launched from Uwch Mynydd by another giant and it still bears his finger marks.

The stones were sometimes erected in pairs and it has often been suggested that they are memorials to a man and his wife.

In a field called Lletfyngharod on Eurglawdd Farm in the parish of Llanfihangel Genau'r Glyn there are two standing stones. There is an ancient prophecy that says when the third stone appears the end of the world is at hand.

Carreg Lefn (The Smooth Stone), near Rhosgoch, Anglesey SH 407903 (114)

A massive standing stone, 12 feet high, which is sometimes referred to as Maen Press (The Brass Stone). It is said to stand near hidden treasure in a brass container which can be found by anyone who traces the shadow made by the stone at a particular time of day.

Another story claims that if you can read an inscription on the stone, it will obligingly move to one side to reveal the treasure. Unfortunately there is no obvious inscription, but natural marks resembling one can be seen.

Ffon y Cawr (Giant's Staff), 1¾ miles west of Roewen, Gwynedd
SH 738717 (115).

This slim, needle-like standing stone can be seen near a cromlech known
as Carn y Bugail. The stone is said to have been thrown there by a giant
from the top of Pen y gaer to wake up his sheepdog, who had gone to sleep
inside the nearby cromlech.

Samson's Stone, near Kenfig, West Glamorgan SS 802838 (170)

St Samson threw this stone to this spot from Margam Mountain. Before cockcrow every Christmas morning it is believed to uproot itself and wander down to the River Sker for a drink.

Garreg y Big (or Llech Bron), near Cross Inn, Dyfed SN 543648 (146)

Standing 14 feet high and 9 feet in diameter at its base, this stone has a pointed top and in the mist it can look like a gigantic figure wrapped in a grey cloak: a strange sight which may well scare any nervous person seeing it for the first time by moonlight. One local story claims that the stone was carried away by the Devil from the top of Trichrug Mountain when he was building his famous bridge across the Afon Mynach (popularly known as the Devil's Bridge). The stone was very heavy, so he sat down to rest for a while until he was startled by the sudden crowing of a cock. He jumped up and fled, leaving the stone behind. His fingerprints may still be seen on the stone if you look carefully – and use your imagination.

The Glasfryn Stone, near Llyn Glasfryn, Lleyn Peninsula, east of
A499 between Llanaelhaearn and Four Crosses, Gwynedd SH
403425 (115)

This stone is associated with the story of a young lady who long ago used
to be the Glasfryn wellkeeper. One day she was careless and forgot to
replace the cover on the well. During the night the water gushed out and
formed a deep lake. For her mistake, the lady wellkeeper was turned into
stone.

Maen y Cleddau (The Sword Stones), near Sylfaen Farm, above Barmouth, Gwynedd SH 632186 (124)

Here can be seen a split rock standing in an enclosure called 'The Field of the Stones'. On each segment of rock is a figure resembling the blade of a sword. Legend tells how Arthur threw his sword against the rock and made the marks.

Another story recalls how long ago someone tried to build a church here, but before it was completed it was destroyed one night by a thunderbolt.

The Dancing Stones of Stackpole. Three stones situated near Samson Farm SM 962963 at Stackpole Warren SM 984946 and in a field near The Home Farm SM 968958 (158)

On a certain day in the year the Dancing Stones of Stackpole are supposed to meet and go down to Rhyd Sais (Saxon's Ford) to dance, and when tired they return to their individual sites. Sometimes, it is said, the Devil accompanies the Dancing Stones on his flute.

Maen Llog, St Mary's Church, Welshpool, Powys SJ 225076 (126)

Standing in the churchyard, this hunk of stone is reputed to have stood formerly in the abbey of Strata Marcella where the abbots were 'installed' on it as part of a well-established ritual. But after the Dissolution of the monasteries, in the reign of King Henry VIII, it was brought here and a new ritual was established. Folk who were required to do penance were made to stand on the stone, dressed in a white sheet, with a candle in one hand. However, the Puritan, Vovasour Powell, had the stone removed from the church because he considered it to be an object of superstition.

When the stone was transferred to the graveyard, where it now stands, it was not long before it took on a new role, as a wishing stone. People would climb on to it and turn around three times to face the sun and make their wish.

The Four Stones, Gwytherin Churchyard, Clwyd SH 876615 (116)

A prehistoric alignment of four stones with one bearing a fifth-century inscription commemorating Vinnemaglus, son of Sennemaglus.

Stone alignments are quite rare in Wales, but one of the most interesting examples can be seen one mile above Llanrhaiadr waterfall in the Tanant valley. It is a double line of stones about 2 feet high, 10 feet apart and 190 feet long, and can be described as a stone avenue.

Parc y Meirw (Field of the Dead), Llanlower, near Fishguard,
Dyfed SM 998359 (157)

Here can be seen an impressive row of eight standing stones, erected over
a distance of 130 feet. Only four of the stones are still standing, but it is the
longest Megalithic alignment in Wales. Stories are told of a ghostly lady in
white being seen near here.

The Three Stones, Trellech, Gwent, SO 498052 (162)

Standing in a field on the outskirts of Trellech, these three stones have been erected in a straight line but they lean in different directions. According to legend, they were thrown there by a giant from the summit of Ysgyryd Fawr about 12 miles away.

The Three Leaps Stones, Pentraeth, off A5025, Anglesey, Gwynedd
SH 529784 (115)

Half a mile from Pentraeth, near the entrance to Plas Gwyn, are three stones in a field where a strange contest is supposed to have taken place in the sixth century.

The daughter of Einion (son of St Geraint) was courted by Hywel (son of Gwalchmai). Another local man also sought her affections, and it was agreed to settle the matter by holding a competition to win her hand in marriage. This was to take the form of a jumping contest and it would be decided by three leaps.

Hywel won by using a hop, skip and jump technique which enabled him to cover about 50 feet. In memory of the occasion, three stones were planted in the ground to mark the length of each leap and they can be seen to this day.

Stone Circles

'Stone circles were originally sited according to some principle which we have yet to rediscover.'

John Michell, The View over Atlantis

There are comparatively few well-known stone circles in Wales and in those that exist the stones are generally quite small in size, being usually about 3 feet to 4 feet in height. Most of the sites are in remote moorland or hillside situations, often close to Bronze Age barrows.

The purpose of the stone circles is still open to conjecture and numerous explanations for their erection have been suggested by archaeologists over the centuries. Some of the circles appear to be associated with burials, for there are cairns built within them, although of course the cairns may have been constructed at a later date within the existing circles.

It has been suggested that they were built as astronomical observatories, or as temples for worshipping the sun god, or that they were once part of a long-forgotten power system.

'The Stone circles, which are usually thought to be temples of some kind, are more probably places where violent dancing in a ring took place to engender power, much in the same way as in electricity a moving coil generates power. The stones were probably put there with the idea of containing the power once it had been generated.'

T. C. Lethbridge

A large number of stone circles have disappeared during the course of time, many having been destroyed through agricultural activities and road building. A large number would have disappeared in early Christian times, for wherever possible they were replaced with the building of a church.

Fedw Circle, near Glascwm in Powys, was once regarded as one of the finest stone circles in Wales. It stands on the highest point of a raised area of peaty land with the ground falling away in all directions.

A plan of the circle published in 1805 in *Archaeologia Cambrensis* shows 27 stones on a true circle with 3 stones outside the circle and another 5 stones inside, making 35 stones altogether. Lieutenant-Colonel Morgan visited the site in 1913 and wrote the following description for the Inventory of Ancient Monuments in the County of Radnor:

'About 30 years ago (about 1880) many stones were removed from the circumference of the circle and some which also stood outside (on account of their being obstacles to the plough) which were placed in groups in their present positions, and others broken up.'

In 1842 a circle of 41 stones was recorded on Bwlch Craigwen in the parish of Penmorfa, Gwynedd. It was oval in shape and measured 66 feet by 54 feet, but during the next seven years it vanished.

Another circle, now vanished, used to stand in the parish of Llandrillo, Gwynedd. It was described in 1842 as 'a circle of stones 12 yards in diameter, within which was formerly a circular cell 6 feet in diameter'.

On Mynydd y Gwyryd in Glamorgan a circle called Carn Llwyd was described in 1842 as a triple concentric circle with an extreme diameter of 65 feet. The medial ring lay 10 feet within this and at the centre was a circular area 7 feet to 8 feet in diameter which may have been a cistvaen. The circle was known locally as Yr Allor (The Altar), but it no longer exists. Two miles to the west of it is the circle of Carn Llechart. (See page 18)

A circle in Llandybie, Dyfed, called Y Naw Carreg (The Nine Stones), was 60 feet in diameter with a central mound.

Hen Dre'r Gelli in the Rhondda Valley was in existence in 1912 and was described as being nearly complete, with a pointer stone, but it no longer exists today.

Several circles have also been destroyed in the Preseli Mountains in Dyfed. Dyffryn Syfynwg was mentioned in 1911 as having a diameter of 78 feet and an inner ring of diameter 40 feet and a central platform 1½ feet to 2 feet high.

At Eithbed in the parish of Maenclochog there were two other circles that were positioned about 100 yards apart. The first one had a diameter of 150 feet and the second one was 120 feet in diameter and surrounded a circular litter of stones, which may have formed an inner ring or a central cromlech. Three other circles once stood at Maenllwyd and Clyn Saithmaen but they also have vanished.

In the parish of Cyffylliog in Gwynedd there used to be a ring work 22 feet in diameter, which was known as Llys Frenhines, 'The Queen's Court'. A boulder called Cader y Frenhines (The Queen's

Chair) was taken from there in 1804, and erected in Pool Park, Ruthin. It resembles an armchair.

The following sites are the best known examples of stone circles to be found in Wales and were described in *Mysterious Wales*:

Y Meini Hirion (Gwynedd), Gray Hill (Gwent), Meini Gwyr, Gors Fawr (Dyfed), Nant Tarw, Cerrig Duon, Yspytty Cynfyn and Old Radnor (Powys). Some of the lesser known sites are featured in the following pages.

Cerrig Gaerall Circles, Powys

Cerrig Gaerall Circles, east of Cemmaes, near Llanbrynmair, Powys SO 904006 (136)

To the south of Llanbrynmair on Newydd Fynyddog hill are two stone circles about 500 feet apart. One is called Cerrig Gaerall and is 69 feet in diameter with just eight stones still standing.

The other circle is called Lled Craenh yr ych (the width of the skin of the ox). Its diameter is 75 feet to 85 feet and there are only three stones left. Another stone can be seen 100 feet outside the circle. It has been estimated that there were once probably fifteen stones in the circle.

According to legend, two ychain bannog (Long-horned oxen of Welsh legend) were separated by the valley of the Twymyn. They stood on top of their respective hills and bellowed until they died of grief because they could not come together. The one which died on Newydd Fynyddog was skinned and his skin marked by the circle of stones spread over the place of interment.

The Fourteen Stones, near Llandrillo, Gwynedd SJ 028387 (125)

In front of Tyfos farmhouse there are fourteen large boulders which form a circle around a raised platform of ground. Few householders can claim to have a prehistoric stone circle in their front gardens!

One and a half miles north-east of Llandrillo, at SJ 056372 (125), is a Bronze Age stone circle, perfect in form with 41 stones in a circle of 36 feet diameter. There is a burial site in the centre.

Stone Circle, about 6 miles south of Holywell and ¼ mile from A541 Clwyd SJ 172679 (116)

The remnants of this stone circle stand in the grounds of Penbedw Park, partially hidden under a clump of trees. Only six stones remain standing.

Ynyshir Circle, Mynydd Eppynt, north of Sennybridge (near Artillery Range!) Powys SN 921383 (160)

The diameter of this remote stone circle was 55 feet to 58 feet and, originally, there would have been 27 stones in position with a wide gap on the south-west side. It is interesting that most of the stone circles on the hills of Wales are composed of small stones.

Carn Llechart, near Pontardawe, West Glamorgan SN 697063 (160)

On Mynydd Llechart (1015 feet) near the summit is a large stone circle, from which the hill takes its name. The circle is nearly complete and, consisting of 24 stones, it has a diameter of 62 feet. Inside the circle is a chambered tomb.

The Fifteen Stones, Bryn Cader Fawr, near Llandecwyn, Gwynedd SH 648354 (124)

On a rocky slope to the west of Moel Ysgyfarnogod is a circle of standing stones 3–4 feet high. If the circle was complete, there would originally have been more than the present 15. In the centre is a rectangular hole about 8 feet by 6 feet, which was probably a burial cist.

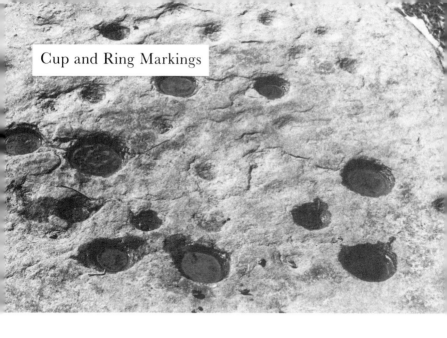

Cup and Ring Markings

These strange markings are often seen on cromlechs, solitary standing stones and rock outcrops. The designs are generally cup-shaped hollows and concentric circles, but spirals and rectangular shapes can sometimes be seen as well. Their purpose and origin is open to conjecture. The amazing thing is that they can be seen on stones in Scotland, Yorkshire, Northumberland and Cornwall. They have even been discovered on rocks in Spain. They remain an unsolved mystery, a Bronze Age riddle.

'Scattered well nigh all over the world, at any rate over the Megalithic world, are found a series of markings which have been called cup and ring markings. They are found only on megaliths or on objects belonging to the Megalithic culture. They are a sign that the object on which they are engraved is holy.'

Gilbert Stone, Wales: her Origins

A boulder at Llanerch Farm in Powys has 31 cups carved on it in 4 rows. The largest number discovered on a single stone in Wales is on a burial chamber near Clynnog fawr, in Gwynedd, where the capstone displays 110 cup markings.

These markings should not be confused with natural hollows caused by water action, for these are generally much deeper and with steeper sides.

Dr Graves, the Bishop of Limerick, remarked about a hundred years ago that, in many cases, the cups were in lines of three, and he put forward the suggestion that they may represent primitive maps showing the locations of ancient burial mounds in the vicinity of the cup and ring-marked stone.

Alternatively, Bishop Browne, in 1919, came to the conclusion that many of the cup marks have been arranged to show patterns of constellations of the heavenly bodies. Another interesting theory was provided by Alfred Watkins (author of *The Old Straight Track*) who suggested that they are direction indicators carved on rocks to show the routes of ancient trackways. Yet another theory is that they indicate the locations of nearby underground springs.

It would certainly seem, from the number of locations, where these markings have been discovered, that they are neither merely ornamental nor freaks of nature, and that the prehistoric people who chiselled them into so many rocks with such evident care and skill must have had some object in doing so. Perhaps one day their meaning will be identified.

Maen Cattwg (Cattwg's Stone), near Gelligaer, Mid Glamorgan
ST 127974 (171)

This squat boulder sits in a field near Heol Adam, a Roman road which leads to the Gaer camp at Brecon. The stone is named after St Cattwg, who spent some time in this vicinity during the late fifth century.

There are several cup marks to be seen on the stone, varying in size and depth. They are dish and conical-shaped holes up to 5 inches in diameter.

Cromlechs, Quoits and Dolmens

'There is no question but that the cromlech is the burial-place of the rich man, and the barrow the burial-place of the poor man.'

Thomas Bateman 1844

The terms cromlech, quoit or dolmen are variously used to describe a stone tomb that has no earth covering mound, the massive capstone and supporting stones being exposed. The word cromlech is Welsh for 'bent flagstone'. They were erected during the period 2000 B.C. to 1500 B.C. and such structures are not only to be seen in the British Isles but also on the Continent and as far east as India and Japan.

Like the pyramids of Egypt, they were constructed as tombs, and in Wales they occur with greater frequency along the coast. Some were built with entrance passages and were constructed in such a way that access was available for later additional burials: these tombs were apparently built as communal burial chambers for use over a long period of time.

Not every person in Neolithic Britain would have been entitled to burial inside a tomb. They were more than likely reserved for the leaders of communities and their families.

These stone structures were originally covered with a large mound of earth or stones that was sometimes circular but more often oval in shape. They may be described as a long barrow or a long cairn if covered with piles of stone instead of earth.

Many cromlechs in Wales are associated in legend with King Arthur, and there are many amazing stories of how they came to be in a particular location. Coetan Arthur (Arthur's Quoit) near Talybont in Gwynedd, for example, was said to have been thrown by Arthur from the summit of Moelfre Hill, and the marks of his fingers, 18 inches long, can still be seen on the stone. Superstitions also associate them with giants, fairies and goblins. They were also once believed to be giants' graves. An alternative theory for their purpose was suggested by fanciful historians in the seventeenth and eighteenth centuries who came to the conclusion that these stone constructions were altar tables that the ancient Druids once used for sacrificial purposes.

Anglesey is the finest area in Wales for studying burial chambers. There are about fifty Neolithic tombs here, far more than in any other part of Wales of comparable size.

Eighteenth-century writers suggested that cromlechs were Druid-ical altars, mainly because they occur so frequently in the areas that were known to be centres of Druidical activity:

'To the lovers of cromlechs and dolmens, and prehistoric camps, Anglesey is a treasure island, and they turn to it with joy; while as the last sanctuary of the Druids it must always, with all its bareness, strike some awe even into the careless mind.'

A. G. Bradley: Highways and Byways in North Wales

Of the numerous cromlechau that are known to have existed on Anglesey, only twenty now remain, and of this number just nine can be said to be in a good state of preservation. The others have shed their capstones, or their supports have collapsed, and in two instances only fragments of the stones remain, while thirteen of the recorded sites have been destroyed completely, leaving no traces.

Unfortunately, hundreds of cromlechs and standing stones must have disappeared over the years. In the reign of William IV the Highway Act of 1835 empowered a road surveyor *'to enter on any waste land or common to dig and search for stone and remove the same. He may also take stones from any river. He may go into another parish and do as above, provided he leave sufficient stone for the said parish. He may enter enclosed land, with consent of the owner, and remove stone, paying nothing for the same, but paying for any damage caused by transportation of the stone. If the owner refuses consent, the surveyor may apply to the nearest justice, who may authorise him to enter the enclosed land to remove any stone he requires.'*

Today, fortunately, we have the Department of the Environment to protect our ancient monuments! In the past, however, farmers were probably pleased to have these 'monstrous' stone relics dyna-mited and cleared off their land. This would not only give them more space for cultivation but also discourage travellers from trespassing to inspect the curiosities.

Arthur's Stone on Cefn Bryn, above Reynoldston, Gower SN
490905 (159)

Otherwise known as Maen Ceti, this cromlech has been described as the
'wonder of the world on Gower'. The raising of the huge stone on to its
supports has also been summed up in ancient records as one of 'the three
arduous undertakings accomplished in Britain'. Hence the proverb: Mal
gwaith Maen Cetti – 'Like the labour of the Stone of Cetti'.

Dyffryn Ardudwy, off A496, about 7 miles north of Barmouth, Gwynedd SH 588228 (124)

Two impressive cromlechs have been exposed by the removal of a massive covering cairn that would, originally, have been about 130 feet long and 55 feet wide. The two burial chambers are about 25 feet apart, and the largest one has a capstone measuring about 10 feet square and nearly 2 feet thick.

Allor Molach (Molach's Altar), on the east side of the River Conwy, Gwynedd SH 793747 (115)

This cromlech, situated in a field above the river near Glan Conwy, has a 22 ton capstone, which is one of the largest in Wales. It has unfortunately slipped out of position.

Pentre Ifan, south-east of Newport, Dyfed SN 099370 (145)

This well-known cromlech is the largest in Dyfed and the second largest in Wales. The massive capstone stands 8 feet above the ground and is high and wide enough to enable six people on horseback to shelter beneath it. Measuring 16 feet long by 9 feet wide, the stone is very impressive.

The cromlech was restored by the Ministry of Works in 1936, when it was in danger of collapsing. Originally, it would probably have been covered by a cairn, estimated at 130 feet long and 65 feet wide at the higher end, where the entrance would have been.

Whether the cromlech/dolmen was or was not covered with an earthen mound is one of the most debated questions of archaeology, and these points are worth considering:

1 The general similarity of these Megalithic chambers makes it highly probable that they were all constructed for one and the same purpose.
2 It seems hard to believe that these structures, which involved so much labour, should have been intended by the builders to be concealed from view.
3 Hundreds of these monuments with no trace of former covering mound can be seen.
4 The builders must have attached considerable importance, and perhaps religious significance, to these structures, for a simple interment could have been effected in a much simpler and less arduous manner.
5 Some of the chambers have holed stones that were surely not intended to be covered up, for the holes, whatever their purpose, would then be of no use.
6 It has been suggested that these monuments were in fact intended to be seen and were constructed as 'mortuary chapels' with their sides filled in with stones.

Whatever their purpose or original form, one must agree that it seems incredible that someone should go to the trouble of raising such masses and poising them on points of stone just for the sake of hiding them again.

2.
Barrows
and Cairns

'. . . the tomen on its lonely hill
Bears silent record of the mighty still!'

Owen Morgan

Ystumcegid Cromlech, Gwynedd

Long Barrows

These consist of burial chambers which have been covered with mounds of earth. However, when large quantities of stone were more readily available the chambers were covered with stones instead and are then referred to as long cairns. They date from Early and Middle Neolithic times (4000 to 2400 B.C.).

It is reasonable to assume that the long barrows were constructed as burial tombs, but many on excavation have been found to contain no evidence of burials. This might suggest that they were sometimes erected for a symbolic purpose to commemorate the dead. They vary considerably in size and design and it should be remembered that over such a long period of time the wind and the rain would have eroded the earth-covering mounds, and originally, therefore, they would have been larger and more impressive.

Many of the chambered barrows and cairns of Wales have at some time been dug out and their contents rifled, leaving empty monuments. For example, the two huge stone cairns of Carneddau Hengwm (see page 32) were opened in the nineteenth century and their contents removed. Bryn yr bobl (The old folks' hill), a mound near Plas Newydd, Anglesey, measuring 150 feet by 100 feet was opened in 1730, but no record of any finds was made.

'Most of our knowledge of the early history of man is derived from the burial remains found in the ancient sepulchres. The burial-places which are called barrows are to be seen all over the world. They are found in North America, Siberia, China and Japan, as well as in Egypt, South America and throughout Europe.'

Gilbert Stone, Wales: her Origins

Neolithic bowl found
in Ty-isaf Long
Barrow

Ty Isaf, near Pengenffordd, A479, Black Mountains, Powys SO 182291 (161)

On the western side of the Black Mountains is a long cairn which is over 100 feet in length and wedge-shaped, being 58 feet wide at its broadest end. There are three chambers inside, where the bones of 33 people were discovered when it was excavated many years ago.

At the south end is a fourth chamber which was found to contain a Bronze Age cremation burial. Of special interest is a false entrance that was cleverly constructed to confuse the tomb robber, for the real entrances were from the sides of the tomb.

Parc le Breos, West Glamorgan

Parc le Breos, near Parkmill, Gower, West Glamorgan SS 537898 (159)

On the west side of Green, Cwm, approached along a track from Parkmill, is one of the finest passage tombs in Wales. It was excavated by Sir John Lubbock in 1869 and by Professor R. J. C. Atkinson in 1960–1, and is in an excellent state of preservation. It is oval in shape, measuring roughly 60 feet by 50 feet. Inside is a passage about 17 feet long and 3 feet wide with small chambers on each side. The remains of twenty bodies were found in the various chambers along with some fragments of Neolithic pottery.

Gwernvale Long Cairn, Powys

Gwernvale Long Cairn, beside A40 on west side of Crickhowell, Powys SO 211192 (161)

Excavation of this site in 1978 by the Clwyd/Powys Archaeological Trust revealed a wedge-shaped cairn nearly 50 yards in length. Three chambers were exposed which contained various Neolithic artefacts, including flint implements, several arrowheads and a stone axe. No human remains were found, but it is likely that they were removed during an earlier excavation in 1804.

Carneddau Hengwm, Gwynedd

Carneddau Hengwm, on a hillside above A496, about 5 miles north of Barmouth, Gwynedd SH 613205 (124)

About 900 feet above sea level is a group of huge burial mounds dating back to the Neolithic Age. They are situated just south of Afon Egryn and difficult to locate, for there are so many stone walls around that the stone cairns, although massive, are hard to see from a distance.

The northern cairn is about 100 feet long and 50 feet wide. Near the centre can be seen the remains of a circular stone wall of about 9 feet in diameter. The capstone that once covered this chamber can be seen near the west end of the cairn and is about 12 feet by 10 feet.

The south cairn would originally have been about 200 feet long by 70 feet wide, but the western end has unfortunately been destroyed. Near the centre is a chamber covered by a large capstone. Access is by a narrow passage, about 3 feet wide, on the north side. The remnants of another chamber can be seen about 30 yards to the east of the middle chamber and it would appear that there were originally at least two other small side chambers as well.

Ty Illtud, Powys

Ty Illtud (The House of Illtud), on Manest Farm near Llanhamlach, east of Brecon, Powys SO 098264 (161)

This chambered cairn is strangely associated with St Illtud who is reputed to be buried at Maen Illtud, a few miles away to the west of Brecon on Mynydd Illtud, near the Brecon Beacons National Park Mountain Centre.

The covering cairn was removed during a nineteenth-century excavation and the flat slabs that form the sides and roof of the chamber have been exposed. More than 60 inscribed crosses and other symbols are visible on the slabs, but they were carved at a much later date than its erection.

It is open to conjecture whether Illtud, who was a contemporary of St David and St Samson, made use of this Neolithic burial chamber as a simple hermit's cell.

Carn Bugail, Cefn Gelligaer, north-west of Bargoed (Mid Glamorgan) ST 101036 (171)

There are two tombs on the summit of this ridge (surmounted by a trig' point) inside an area of about 50 feet in diameter. There used to be two chambers, within a heap of stones, lined with large stone slabs but there is little to be seen now, for they were excavated and robbed during the nineteenth century.

Another tomb a few miles away at Lancaith Isaf Farm was excavated in the 1930s by Sir Mortimer Wheeler. Inside, he found a beaker and the skeleton of a child. Some marks on the skull showed evidence of the youngster having suffered from rickets. Sir Mortimer described his find:

'The earliest case of the disease known in Britain or probably in the world!'

33

Round Barrows

It was the Beaker people who introduced the technique of single burials in round mounds, abandoning the old system of communal burials in huge stone cromlechs which obviously required an enormous amount of labour to construct. They were constructed during the period 2100 to *c* 700 B.C.

The corpse was placed in a cist (a surrounding of large flat stones) on its side, with the knees tucked up under the chin in the crouched attitude of sleep. A covering mound was then constructed, about 6 feet high and often 70 feet across. The dead person was often provided with various items that might be required in the afterlife; these generally included a pottery beaker of food or drink and sometimes an arrowhead.

A later development was the introduction of cremation. The body was burnt to ashes on a funeral pyre and the ashes and burnt bones were then placed in an urn (a rough-shaped crock 12 to 18 inches high and decorated with patterns), accompanied by pieces of jewellery and various weapons. The urn would then be placed, inverted, in a stone surround (cist) and a large barrow or cairn raised over it. A symbolic protective trench was sometimes cut around the mound. No entrance passages were provided to the barrows or cairns, for they were intended as solitary and permanent burial mounds.

'The attitude of primitive man to the spirits of the dead is complex; it is a compound of hope and fear, of affection and aversion, of attraction and repulsion, and in any attempt to analyse it, full account should be taken of all these conflicting emotions and tendencies.'

Sir James Frazer,
The Fear of the Dead in Primitive Religion

A beaker discovered near Penderyn in Powys

The Beaker people were the first Bronze Age immigrants in about 2400 B.C. They were named after their pots or beakers which have been found in so many of their grave mounds.

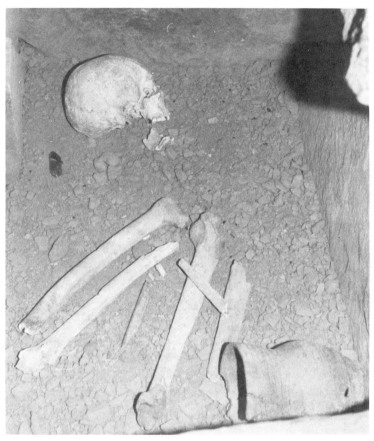

The Brymbo Beaker and burial. National Museum of Wales, Cardiff, South Glamorgan

A round barrow excavated at Merthyr Mawr, West Glamorgan in 1919 contained six crouched skeletons and three beakers, which were all remarkably uniform in design. The only handled beaker found in Wales was at Pen Gloch y pibwr in the Black Mountains, Powys.

Food vessels also accompanied the unburnt burials of the Bronze Age and were sometimes associated with cremation as well. The vessel was presumably placed in the grave to hold food for the deceased. The vessels were not as tall as the beakers, measuring only 4 to 6 inches in height.

Cinerary urns were generally much larger than the beakers and food vessels. They were often made of a coarse ware, the clay having been mixed with stone and sand. Many of them are ornamented with dots and lines and, very often, chevron patterns. The ornamentation was generally restricted to the upper part of the vessel.

3.
Mystic Mounds –
The Pyramids of Wales

'The people who honoured us with their presence here in Britain some four thousand years ago had evidently, some way or other, had communicated to them a very complete Egyptian culture.'

Sir Norman Lockyer

Large mound near St Illtud's Church, Llanhilleth, Gwent

One of the great mysteries of Wales is the number of massive mounds that bear no resemblance to barrows and are often identified in local folklore as ancient burial mounds or conveniently categorized as castle mounds by the archaeologist or historian. These large manmade heaps occur frequently throughout Wales and are very often situated near churches.

The big question is – were the great mounds erected for burial purposes or were they later utilized as such, for it is strange that many of the mounds and barrows of Britain when excavated showed no evidence of burials having taken place. It is perhaps of parallel significance that the Great Pyramid of Egypt has always been regarded as a tomb for an Egyptian king, yet no body has ever been discovered inside it.

Were the chambers within some of the artificial mounds, such as Bryn Celli Du, built and used for some mysterious and long forgotten purpose? It has been suggested that perhaps they were constructed as initiation chambers, where strange ceremonies took place, or perhaps as energy accumulators associated with a long-forgotten energy system as suggested by the dowser B. Tomkins:

'. . . every hill and dale, dotted over with electric waving mounds precisely over each fountain head while connected with most of these magnetic mounds are electric currents waving on the earth's surface over the exact track of every subterranean water course.'

Mounds where no burials have been found should perhaps be regarded as cenotaphs, symbolic monuments to the memory of the dead – the larger the mound the greater the person. Many large mounds throughout Wales have been identified as Norman mottes, but it is quite possible that a considerable number of them were originally burial or monumental mounds that were then used by the Normans as the bases for their defensive mottes. On the border of Wales at St Weonards (Herefordshire) a flat topped castle-mound near the church was excavated in 1855 by Thomas Wright, who declared on the 'testimony of the spade' that it was originally a prehistoric grave hill.

The ruins of St Ffraed's chapel in Anglesey stand on a large artificial mound. In the eighteenth century it was breached by a violent storm that exposed a large number of skeletons placed in tiers with their heads towards the west. They were all males and it may be assumed that they were slain in a battle.

Twm Barlwm, above Risca, Gwent ST 244926 (171)

A very impressive mound on the summit of this hill is known locally as 'the pimple' and, according to local stories, handed down through the ages, an important Celtic chief is supposed to be buried inside the mound.

Historians disagree and maintain that it was constructed by the Normans as a motte. It is impossible, however, that both theories are correct, for perhaps the mound, like many others of similar position and character in this part of Wales, was constructed as a monumental tomb and later converted by the Normans into a motte.

Twyn Tudor, Mynyddislwyn, Gwent ST 193938 (171)

There are various legends associated with this mysterious mound which stands near Mynyddislwyn church. One story recalls how a Roman army was overwhelmed by a vast horde of Celts and the slaughtered legionaries were buried beneath this huge mound. It has been suggested, alternatively, that it is the monumental grave mound of an early British king.

Gop Hill, near Trelawnyd, off A5151, Clwyd SH 086802 (116)

Dominating Trelawnyd village is Gop Hill, a conspicuous landmark that rises to an altitude of 820 feet. On the summit is an enormous cairn constructed of limestone. This is believed to be the largest artificial mound in Wales. It measures about 330 feet across and is about 50 feet high.

Professor Boyd Dawkins carried out excavations here in 1886. He sank a central shaft right down to the bedrock, but his efforts were not rewarded with any significant finds. However, further down the hill below this cairn, he excavated a cave and discovered a small sealed chamber cut into the limestone. Inside were fourteen skeletons in crouched positions, with their arms and legs drawn together and folded. Of particular interest is the fact that the shape of their skulls showed two different periods of man, thought to be Neolithic and Early Bronze Age. Fragments of crude pottery and flint tools were also found here.

Ynysycrug Mound before 1855. This Mound was about
100 feet high.

Ynysycrug (Field of the Mound), Glyn Rhondda, Mid Glamorgan SS 994928 (170)

This large mound was partially removed in 1855 when a railway was being constructed. Less than one-sixth of the original structure remained and, originally, it was probably nearly 100 feet high. It is said that when the workmen dug into the mound they found it to be swarming with snakes.

Dr William Price, a Llantrisant eccentric, organized a group of men to dig into the mound in 1870 in the hope of finding treasure. Soon after they started, the sky darkened, lightning flashed and the rain came down in torrents, causing the men to down their spades and flee in terror.

Carn y Gelyn (The Cairn of the Enemy), above Penygraig in the Rhondda area, Mid Glamorgan SS 976906 (170)

This enormous mound was constructed of countless millions of tons of earth and stones which must have been transported there in primitive carts, for 100 yards above the mound is an enormous cutting running behind the brow of the hill. Its entire length is strewn with stones and it may be conjectured that the material for the mound came from this site. One can imagine thousands of men working furiously to entomb the bodies of a defeated enemy – possibly Roman soldiers who were defeated in a great battle in this area. The very name of Carn y Gelyn has a ring of triumph about it.

Other names in the area that tie in with the theory of a great battle taking place here are:
Tyle'r Gelyn (Ascent of the Enemy)
Cil y Meirch (The Ravine of the War Horses)

41

The Devil's Mound, near Llandyssul, Dyfed SN 383392 (143)

Between Landyssul and Llangeler is a large mound known as Cnw Coedfael which is attributed to the activities of the Devil. He was taking a huge load of earth on his shoulder to fill in the Teifi and drown the people of Pentre Cwrt who were too virtuous for his liking. On the way he met a cobbler from Llandyssul who was carrying a sackful of worn shoes to mend.

The cobbler, aware of the Devil's intentions, told him that it was a long way to Pentre Cwrt and that he had himself worn out a sackful of shoes in getting there. So the Devil laid down his huge load and went away. Hence the mound!

Romano-British Burial Mounds

> *'. . . the carnedd on the lonely hill*
> *Bears silent record of the mighty still.'*

> *F. Henman*

Of particular interest in ancient Welsh literature are the Englyn y Beddau and Englynion Beddau Milwyr ynys Prydain (The stanzas of the tombs and stanzas of the tombs of the British warriors).

This is a collection of traditional verses relating to the graves of about 200 persons who had distinguished themselves for good or evil reasons in the history of their people from the earliest remembered times until the end of the sixth century. Generally, the graves mentioned in the stanzas are situated on hilltops, near seashores, on the banks of rivers or in churchyards.

For example:

> *Gwydion ab Don's tomb is said to be on*
> *Morfa Dinllen (the shore of Dinllen);*
> *that of Bedwyr is on Allt Tryvan – the slope*
> *of Tryfa; Rhun is buried near Llan Rhydnant*
> *(on the bank of the Llydnant) and Dylan in Llanfeuno – (Beuno's church).*

This early poetry provides an indication that the practice of interring in cairns and barrows on hills and plains continued right up to the sixth century.

> *'Whose is the tomb on the mountain?*
> *His, who commanded hosts;*
> *It is the tomb of Teyrnvae Hael ab Hywlydd.'*

And:

> '*Whose is the tomb under the hill?*
> *It is the tomb of a warrior in Cyvysgyn*
> *The tomb of Cynon son of Clydno Eiddyn.*'

Clydno Eiddyn was a chief of North Britain and is said to have been one of the three counselling warriors of Arthur.

In Llywarch Hen's *Elegy* we are informed that one of his sons was buried on a mountain and in the next line another son is described as being located in a church:

> '*The tomb of Gwell is in Rhiw Felin*
> *The tomb of Sawyl is in Llangollen.*'

It seems that following the introduction of Christianity and the erection of a large number of churches, there was a change in burial customs and churchyard interments became the custom.

> '*The grave of Pryderi is at Abergynolwyn*
> *where the torrents rush from the mountains;*
> *The grave of Gwallawg the Tall*
> *is on the banks of the brook of Carrog.*'

It has been claimed that the sepulchral urn of Pryderi is located in the Vale of Llanegrin where the waters of Cynolwyn join with the Diswnwy at Abergynolwyn.

The grave of Gwallawg the Tall is declared to be on the banks of the brook of Carrog (Gwynedd). About 100 yards from where the road from Llandwnog Church to Caernarvon crosses the Carrog, there is a circular mound and here in the last century a British urn was found which may have contained the ashes of Gwallawg ap Llenawg.

Llenawg was one of the native princes of Cumbria who fought under the banner of Caswallon Law Hir and helped to expel the Irish from Môn and Arfon.

Near Trelech in Dyfed is an immense cairn which is often referred to as Crug Edeyrn and it is reputed that Edeyrn is buried here. A cistfaen was opened in 1830 and coloured bones and charcoal were found inside.

According to William of Malmesbury, the tomb of Gwalchmai was discovered in 1086 on the sea shore at Rhôs in Dyfed. In the Welsh Triads Gwalchmai is mentioned as one of the three golden-tongued knights in the court of Arthur. His castle was at Castell Gwalchmai (Walwyn's Castle) in Dyfed.

A tumulus known as Yr Gorsedd Wen is reputed to be the burial place of Gwen, who was one of the sons of Llywarch Hen: 'on the ford of Morlas was slain Gwen'.

The mound is 26 yards in diameter and 6 feet high and it is located in a field near the river Morlas. In 1851 it was excavated and a skeleton of a man 'impressive in stature' was found deep in the centre of the tumulus.

To the north of Gwent, beyond the Monnow, was the ancient kingdom of Erging or Archenfield. This is now a part of Herefordshire, but it was once a part of Wales and was named after the Roman fort of Ariconium, located at Weston under Penyard. A mound situated near a spring called Licat Amir – 'the eye of Amir' – was said to contain the remains of one of King Arthur's sons who was killed by Arthur himself and buried here. Nennius, writing in the ninth century, supplies the following description of the mound:

'The man who is buried in the tump was Amir. And men came to measure the tump, it sometimes measures in length seven feet, sometimes fifteen feet, and sometimes nine feet. Whatever measure you may make it at one time you will not again find it the same measurement.'

'The soil of Wales is the dust of patriots.'

Marie Trevelyan

The Grave of Sawyl Benisel, on Allt Cynadda to the north of Kidwelly, West Glamorgan SN 406088 (159)

This site is located on a hill (Allt Cynadda – derived from a British prince) near a farm to the north of Kidwelly. Here can be seen an ancient encampment with two tumuli to the north-east of it. The larger of the two is about 300 yards from the camp and measures 56 feet in diameter. It was excavated in 1850. The diggers came across a large flat stone (at a depth of 2 feet) cut into a hexagonal shape resembling an ancient shield. It was 8 feet 4 inches in length, and 7 feet across and from 12 inches to 15 inches thick. The cist was located below it and this was found to contain a tall and complete skeleton lying on its back. It appeared to have received a blow on the left side – possibly from a sling shot or a hefty weapon.

It has been suggested that this is the grave and skeleton of Sawyl Benisel who was killed in an attack on his camp and buried here by the enemy who stripped him of all his ornaments and weapons. If he had been on the winning side, it is probable that he would have been buried inside the camp and not outside it.

According to the lists of the kings of ancient Britain, Sawyl Benisel (the father of St Asaf), known as 'the high headed or arrogant', succeeded Rhydderch, and was himself succeeded by Pyr. The burial mound used to be known as Banc Benisel and a hill in the neighbourhood is called Mynydd Penisel (Penisel's Mountain). Nearby is a holy well which used to be known as Ffynnon Sel which is probably a corruption of Benisel.

'The warrior or the bard fell, and the cairn arose upon his grave to point out his resting-place for ever. The mist enshrouds it, the wind plays its requiem over it, the unearthly roars and moans and music of the elements have acted like a charm upon the manes of the Celtic dead, so as to rivet them to their mountains.'

David Lloyd Isaac, Silvriana

Twmpath Diwlith (The Dewless Mound), Mynydd Margam, east of Port Talbot, West Glamorgan SS 832887 (170)

High on the slopes of Mynydd Margam this tumulus is the location where the Bodvoc Stone used to stand (see page 98). According to tradition, no dew ever falls on this mound, which used to be regarded as one of the seven wonders of Glamorgan.

There are many other tumuli in this vicinity. Two of them are called Yr Ergyd Uchaf (The Highest Blow) and Yr Ergyd Isaf (The Lowest Blow). These mounds are said to be the burial-places of the dead who fell in battles fought on these hills.

'The many cairns or graves on the Alps of Glamorgan serve the purpose of milestones and finger posts to the befogged or benighted traveller.'

John Griffith, 1904

The tumulus of Eliseg, near the ruins of Valle Crucis Abbey, Clwyd
SJ 203445 (117)

The pillar of Eliseg stands on a small tumulus near the A542 road. The inscribed pillar stone was erected by Concenn (or Cyngen) in the ninth century as a memorial to his great-grandfather Eliseg, who was killed while fighting off the Saxons and buried within his own territory. In 1803 the tumulus was excavated and the following description is an account of the possible discovery of the bones of King Eliseg:

'On digging below the flat pedestal in which the base of the pillar had been inserted, they came to a layer of pebble stones; and, after having removed them, to a large flat slab on which it seems the body had been laid as they now found the remains of it, guarded round with large flat blue stones and covered at top with the same; the whole forming a sort of stone box or coffin. The bones were entire and of very large dimensions. The skull and teeth which were very white and perfect were particularly sound . . . By this it should seem that Eliseg was not an old man when he was buried here and it is wonderful that greater decomposition had not taken place in twelve hundred years.'

Archaeologia Cambrensis

It is not certain, however, that Eliseg's pillar stands on its original site, for it was thrown down during the Civil War and broken into two pieces. In 1779, Mr Lloyd of Trevor Hall erected the upper part of the pillar (displaying sixteen lines of inscription, see page 124) upon its original base and set it up on the tumulus where it now stands, but it is possible that the burial dates back to the Bronze Age.

The Tall Men of Tal-y-Llyn, near B4405, south of Cader Idris, Dolgellau, Gwynedd SH 720100 (124) approx.

Some enormous coffins were found in 1684 near Tal-y-Llyn lake, and inside were the skeletons of very tall men. Beside them were hazel rods. Bearing this in mind, the following statement, written by Carmoc Prince, Bishop of Castel in the ninth century, is of particular interest:

'A wooden rod was used for measuring corpses and graves, and this rod used to be kept in the burial places of the heathen, and it was an honour to everyone even to touch it; and whatever was abominable they (the pagans) used to inscribe on this stick in Ogham.'

Ogham writing (see page 90) is a script peculiar to the early Irish and consists of angled strokes on a stick or a slab of stone. The script is only found in Ireland, Scotland, Wales (especially South Wales) and in Devon and Cornwall, where the Irish established settlements.

Bryn yr Ellyllon (Hill of the Goblins), near Mold on the A541, Clwyd. Destroyed.

There used to be a burial mound near Mold that had the reputation of being haunted. Local people used to claim that if you looked towards the barrow at a certain time of night you would see a man on a horse wearing gold armour. He would beckon to people and try to lead them away from the mound.

In 1833, however, the mound was excavated:

'When more than three hundred loads of stone had been carted away the workmen came to the skeleton of a tall and powerful man placed at full length. He had been laid there clad in a finely-wrought corslet of gold, with a lining of bronze: the former was found to be a thin plate of the precious metal, measuring three feet seven inches long by eight inches wide. Near at hand were discovered 300 amber beads and traces of something made of iron, together with an urn of ashes, and standing about three yards from the skeleton.'

See page 214 for additional information.

Professor Rhys
Celtic Britain

It was at the time suggested that this is the grave of Benlli Gawr whose name is remembered by the hill fort of Moel Fenlli, a few miles to the west of Mold. The grave of his son Beli, who was a great war leader, is mentioned in the following stanza from the Black Book of Carmarthen:

> *Pieu yr bed yn y Maes Mawr,*
> *Balch y law ar a lafnawr?*
> *Bet Beli ab Benlli Gawr.*

> Whose the grave in the Great Plain,
> Proud his hand on his weapon?
> Beli's grave, son of Benlli the Giant.

The 'Great Plain' was possibly Maes Mawr to the east of Moel Fammau, a few miles away. Beli fell fighting Meirion (of Merioneth). He was buried with two stones placed at each end of his grave. They were still in place in the sixteenth century, according to the Welsh scholar of that period – John Jones of Gelli Lyfdy. A brook nearby was known as Nany y Meini, 'The Brook of the Stones'.

The mound has now, unfortunately, disappeared following development of the area, but the golden cape may be seen in the British Museum in London. A facsimile of it may also be seen in the National Museum of Wales, Cardiff.

Mound digging and tomb robbing were once popular pastimes in Victorian times, but unfortunately were not usually carried out very carefully or scientifically, and the finds were generally kept by the diggers as souvenirs and subsequently either destroyed or misused.

'About two miles from Caerphilly . . . are several tumuli, in which burnt bones have been found, but no medals. They were opened about the year 1752 . . . The urns were all broken by the workmen.'

B. H. Malkin, Scenery, Antiquities of South Wales

There are many tales throughout Wales of tomb plunderers being frightened away by torrential rain and great flashes of lightning and deafening thunder. One such story concerns a man who was digging at Cae Adda in Mathafarn in Powys, where there are two parallel rows of mounds. It was not long before he was driven away by heavy rain from a clear sky. A few days later he tried again but was forced to retreat under a fall of hailstones. At his third attempt, lightning frightened him away. In a fit of temper and exasperation he threw down his spade and never returned.

A more recent story concerns the large mound on Twm Barlwm, near Risca in Gwent, where, according to local stories, an important British chieftain is supposed to be buried, although historians claim that the mound is really an eleventh-century motte constructed by the Normans. The mound has been badly eroded over the years by the trampling of countless feet, by wind and rain, and by vandalism by motorcycle scramblers. In 1984, Gwent County Council set up a scheme in conjunction with the Manpower Services Commission to renovate the mound. This involved repairing the erosion, returfing the sides, raising the height of the mound, constructing a flight of steps to the top, and erecting a fence around the base to keep out the motorcyclists.

On Monday 4 June, 1984, Terry Wilmot, the team supervisor, wrote the following report on the day's activities:
'At about 1.00 P.M., while myself and my men were working on Twm Barlwm, constructing steps, a long swarm of bees forced us to stop work for about twenty minutes. Where they came from I don't know. All I know is that they were about thirty feet from us at the

south end of the mound and it was just like a long black cloud. After about twenty minutes they went away and we then continued working. At about 1.45 P.M. I went down to the van and as I got to the driving door I found that the side of the van was half covered with a swarm of bees.'

There are stories of other people in the distant past being disturbed by swarms of bees on Twm Barlwm and the following quotation is relevant:

'Sometimes this awful labour (the removal of cromlechs in Wales) is accompanied by fierce storms of hail and wind, or violent lightning; sometimes by mysterious noises, or swarms of bees which are supposed to be fairies in disguise . . .'

Wirt Sikes,
British Goblins

4.
Hill Forts, Ancient Settlements and Lake Dwellings

'You cannot live in the present – at least not in Wales.'

R. S. Thomas

Pen y Gaer, north-east of Llanidloes, overlooking the Clywedog
reservoir, Powys SN 908869 (136)

On the summit of this Iron Age hill fort there are vast numbers of stones
that once formed a defensive wall around the summit of the hill. Local
legend claims that they were dropped there by a giantess who had gathered
them in her apron for building her house. As in many similar stories
around Wales, the apron strings broke and the stones were scattered
around the hill.

Hill Forts

In Britain there are approximately 3000 hill forts to be seen and about 200 of these are located in Wales. The Welsh forts are not, as it first appears, haphazardly placed but are located in well-defined groups, closely associated with valley and coastal routes. They often overlook fording places in valleys and occupy commanding positions, and are sometimes situated near ancient trackways.

The majority of hill forts are fascinating places to visit. One can not fail to be impressed with the extent of the fortifications or the great labour that must have been involved in their construction. They provide splendid vantage points, offering panoramic views and a walk to the summit plateau may involve a steep and challenging ascent. The majority of these forts date from the Iron Age, 450 B.C. to 43 A.D. The size of the forts varies from 600 acres to just over one acre.

They were constructed as the tribal central headquarters where the chieftain resided with his family and followers. In times of emergency the other members of the tribe would seek refuge in the fort and help to defend the extensive rampart fortifications when the enemy was attacking. It is not hard to imagine the bloodthirsty battles that must have been fought on these defensive positions between the warring tribes or against the armies of Rome. Stones were hurled from slings on to the heads of the attackers and showers of spears and arrows filled the air.

Some of the forts are up to 3500 years old and the locations were well chosen, always taking advantage of any natural defensive opportunity where a cliff, a river or the sea provided protection on at least one side. The early forts had only one ring of ramparts (e.g. Table Mountain, see page 53) but later ones such as Llanmelin in Gwent (page 60) had a series of ring defences and well-protected and elaborate entrances.

In some locations concentric ramparts, following the contours of the hilltop, provide a series of defensive positions; they were sometimes constructed of dry stone walling to form a very substantial fortification (for example, Caer y Tŵr – Anglesey, Tre'r Ceiri – Lleyn Peninsula, and Garn Goch – Dyfed). On other sites the ramparts were earthen, possibly with timber palisades. In some instances there would have been over a mile of rampart to defend, and it is interesting to consider how many men would have been

Crug Hywel (otherwise known as Table Mountain), near
Crickhowell, Powys SO 225206 (161)

The town of Crickhowell takes its name from this hill fort which overlooks
the town and is associated with Hywel ap Rhys of Morgannwg, and not
Hywel Dda as is generally supposed.

The fort is of a simple design with only one rampart and it is probably a
very early fortified site.

involved in providing sufficient cover.

One should take into consideration, when looking at the altitude
of some of these citadels, that in those far off times the climate was
possibly warmer than today with less rainfall, allowing people to
live in relative comfort on the hilltops.

It has been shown by certain excavations that these forts were in
use for centuries and then abandoned for periods, later to be
restored and brought back into operation, no doubt against a new
enemy such as the Romans during the period 50–75 A.D. When the
Romans had firmly established control over Wales, the forts must
have largely fallen into disuse.

In Gwent, Llanmelin and Sudbrook forts were abandoned when
the civil town of Isca Silurum (Caerwent) was constructed by the
Romans and the local Silures were enticed into enjoying the

advantages of the Roman way of life, with the availability of shops, baths, drinking houses, underfloor heating and various forms of entertainment.

There is evidence to show that when the Romans departed, many of the hill forts were brought back into use. This was the era of the Dark Ages when the Saxon hordes were causing problems and the local chieftains or rulers of the petty kingdoms of Wales restored many of the hilltop fortresses. It is unfortunate that so few of these hilltop citadels have been excavated, for they should reveal some fascinating discoveries and could provide more information on the sixth-century Arthurian period when some of these forts were re-occupied. Y Breidden in Montgomeryshire has been partially excavated and finds here show that the fort was re-occupied in the late fourth century when a number of huts were constructed. One of the most interesting finds was a sixth-century silver brooch.

Carn Ingli, above Newport, Dyfed SN 062372 (145)

Here on the edge of the Preseli hills is a spectacular Iron Age hill fort where a massive tumble of stones marks the line of the ancient ramparts. The sites of numerous circular huts can be seen inside the enclosure.

This site is an excellent viewpoint, well worth the walk involved in reaching it; on a clear day it is possible to see Ireland.

Garn Fawr, near Strumble Head, west of Fishguard, Dyfed SM 895388 (157)

Impressively situated on a headland above Pwll Deri (Youth Hostel) is one of the finest stone forts in Britain. A track leads up to it from a small car park at SM 898387. From the trig' point on the summit of this fort is a magnificent view across Pwll Deri to the headland beyond. On a clear day one can see the Wicklow hills in Ireland, Snowdon and the Lleyn Peninsula in North Wales.

Foeldrygarn (Hill of Three Cairns), near Crymmych, eastern end of Mynydd Preseli, Dyfed SN 158336 (145)

Inside the enclosure of this hill fort are three large cairns which are said to be the burial sites of three kings – Môn, Maelan and Madog.

This is a common feature to many hill forts and similar cairns can be seen on other forts in the Preseli hills area; for example, Foel Foeddau, Mynydd Cilciffaeth and Freni Fawr.

Bwrdd Arthur (Arthur's Table), 3 miles west of Penmon on Anglesey, Gwynedd SH 585814 (115)

The summit of this hill fort (which is also sometimes referred to as Din Silwy) is 500 feet above sea level. It is fortified by a stone wall, faced inside and outside with stone slabs. Inside the huge enclosure on the hilltop are traces of circular stone huts.

If your imagination is working well, look out for a circular stone resembling a table with 24 'seats' around it – it has been labelled King Arthur's Round Table.

Garn Goch, between Llandeilo and Llangadoch, Dyfed SN 685244 (159)

Garn Goch is rated as one of the finest prehistoric hill forts in Britain, and it is the largest in Wales. It consists of two forts situated side by side – Y Gaer Fach and Y Gaer Fawr (The Small Fort and The Big Fort). The larger fort has a rubble wall surrounding it, over 600 yards in length, enclosing an area of about 200 yards wide. In 1892 some pieces of pottery and a flint arrowhead were found here.

The situation of the two forts provides a commanding view over the surrounding country, and any enemy approaching from the low-lying course of the Tywi would be easily sighted.

At the south-east end of the upper fort is a cairn of stones about 30 feet in diameter which, on excavation, revealed a small cist showing signs of cremation. There are numerous grave mounds within the walls of the camp, varying in shape from oblong to circular.

The lower fort consists of a wall built around the crown of the hill. It is oval in form and about 500 feet from west to east and 350 feet from north to south with the main entrance at its eastern end.

Castell Dinas, east of Newport, A487, Dyfed SN 116391 (145)
Postal address: Pant Glas, Meline, Crymych, Dyfed

This promontory fort was occupied mainly in the Iron Age and the Romano-British period when the Demetae tribe lived here from about the second to the fourth century A.D.

In recent years the fort has been carefully excavated and it is now open to the public at Easter, late Spring holiday and from mid-July to the end of August. School visits at other times can be arranged in advance.

Hundreds of volunteers have been involved in the project, labouring in all kinds of weather conditions, to uncover the story of the occupation of this fascinating site. There is much to see here, including the reconstruction of an Iron Age roundhouse which would have occupied the site some 2000 years ago.

The construction of this hut was begun at the time when Prince William of Wales was born, so the archaeologists working at Castell Henllys decided to dedicate their building to the young prince. They claim that the hut should last for at least one hundred years, but a new thatch roof is likely to be required within fifty years. Oak from Pengelly forest, about a mile away, was used for the main timbers. Hazel and willow, obtained from the estate, were used for the purlins. The reeds for thatching the roof came from the Nevern Estuary. Unfortunately, this supply was exhausted and the top section of the roof was ultimately thatched with reeds imported from Hungary. It took 4½ tons of reed to complete the roof and involved 660 hours of work. The walls of the hut were covered in a mixture of mud, horse hair and cow dung.

A section cut into the ramparts of the fort shows clearly how the bank was supported by stones and boulders which were brought on to the site for that purpose. Stone walls were constructed on each side of the ramparts and the area behind the main defences was thus fairly well sheltered from the wind and rain, so this was an ideal location for the tribe to build their houses and stores. Excavations have shown the sites of several buildings and reddened areas of earth indicate the fire hearths.

Excavations have also shown evidence of the existence of a furnace which would have been used for making bronze or iron, so it is possible that Castell Henllys was once an important centre of industrial activity.

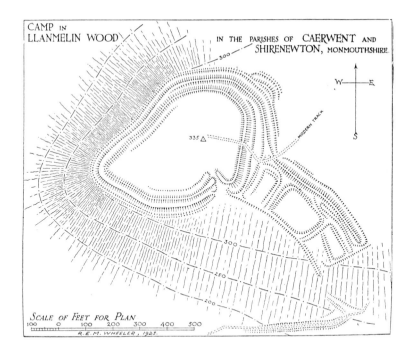

CAMP in LLANMELIN WOOD IN THE PARISHES OF CAERWENT AND SHIRENEWTON, MONMOUTHSHIRE.

335 △

SCALE OF FEET FOR PLAN
100   0   100   200   300   400   500

R.E.M. WHEELER, 1923.

Llanmelin Hill Fort, north of Caerwent, Gwent ST 451926 (171)

This small but elaborate fort with multiple ramparts dates back to the later part of the Early Iron Age. It was occupied by the Silures who offered very determined resistance during the Roman invasion, although they were eventually persuaded to leave their hilltop settlement and live lower down at Caerwent, which the Romans constructed as a Civil town called Venta Silurum – 'Market Town of the Silures'. Here the tribe could live, serving their Roman masters, in a new style of luxury with comfortable houses, public baths, shops, and inns. In the church of Caerwent there is an interesting inscribed stone which refers to RESPUBLICA CIVITATIS SILURIUM – 'The Commonwealth of the Silures'.

Their hill fort was a roughly elliptical enclosure measuring 750 feet by 500 feet with an internal area of nearly 5½ acres. On one side of the camp is a narrow oblong 'annexe' measuring 400 feet by 230 feet, covering an area of 2¼ acres.

The camp is 340 feet above sea level and it was defended by a multiple series of banks and ditches with a single entrance near the junction of the main camp and the annexe.

60

Clegyr Boia, to the west of St David's, Dyfed SM 744252 (157)

This small fort is situated on the summit of a large mass of igneous rock which rises about 45 feet above the surrounding farmland and is roughly 320 feet long by 100 feet wide.

The illustration shows how the summit has been fortified by a bank of stones mingled with earth. Originally, the bank would have been faced on both sides with large slabs set on end, in a similar fashion to the camp of Bwrdd Arthur on Anglesey (see page 56). Most of the facing stones at Clegyr Boia have been removed for building purposes, but some still remain in place.

The camp is roughly a rectangular parallelogram with an outpost on the north-eastern extremity. The interior of the main camp and the annexe have been hollowed out, and these excavations have, of course, provided the stone and earth to build the ramparts.

In the sixth century the site was occupied by Boia, a Gwyddel chief who gave St David considerable problems, although the latter eventually dealt with him by causing fire to fall from heaven and consume the fortress.

There is reputed to be a well here that is a small hollow in the rock, just large enough for a fist to be inserted. It is claimed that the water is good for soothing sore eyes.

Caerau, near Llantrisant, Mid Glamorgan SS 065833 (170)

Caerau hill fort is one of the largest and most perfect camps in Wales. It is nearly circular in form with triple defences and is 549 feet above sea level at its highest point, providing extensive views in all directions. This isolated hill is oval in shape, but the fort itself is nearly circular with its strongest defences on the west side with double ramparts and a broad outer bank. On the north side there are triple defences consisting of three banks and two ditches. The bank on the south-east side was built of dry stone walling with a backing of earth.

Caerau (the plural of caer) is derived from cae – a field enclosed with hedges. Camp is a Saxon word which comes from the Latin campus.

Bryn Euryn, near Colwyn Bay, off A55, Gwynedd SH 833798 (116)

The summit of this 428 feet hill is marked by a hill fort and in the hollow on the top can be seen several burial mounds and the sites of hut circles. A curving line of rubble was once a stone rampart enclosing the top of the hill. This was a very good defensive position, with a steep slope on the southern side and a valley below which is now the route of the road to Conwy. It was in this valley of Nant Semper that the Roman General Sempronius was ambushed and killed.

Caergai (Kei's Fortress) near Bala, Gwynedd SH 877314 (125)

On a gentle slope overlooking Llanuwchllyn, near the A494, is this ancient stronghold which is associated with Cai Hir (Tall Cai) and his father Cynyr Farfog (the bearded) who was said to be King Arthur's foster father.

In earlier times this was also the site of a Roman fort and the summit is now occupied by an eighteenth-century farmhouse, but earthworks and remains of stone walls can be seen nearby.

Pen Dinas, near Aberystwyth, Dyfed SN 584805 (135)

Is situated 400 feet above the Rheidol and Ystwyth rivers. It is an unusual fort shaped like an hourglass with clearly defined ramparts. On the site stands a nineteenth-century column erected by a local squire in honour of the Duke of Wellington.

Pen-y-Crug in Powys SO 029303 (160

Overlooks the town of Brecon and provides an excellent viewpoint of the Brecon Beacons. Its summit covers an area of five acres and it is defended by three sets of banks and ditches with an entrance on the south side.

Carn Fadryn, 4 miles south of Nevin, Lleyn Peninsula, Gwynedd SH 278352 (123)

On the summit of this cone-shaped hill is an ancient fortress, similar to that of Tre'r Ceiri (a few miles away), with extensive stone ramparts and remains of stone hut circles. A large flat stone on the summit called Bwrdd y Brenin (The King's Table) is supposed to conceal a pot of gold.

Din Lligwy, near Moelfre, east side of Anglesey, Gwynedd SH 496862 (114)

This is the finest example in Wales of a group of fourth-century hut circles, situated within a walled enclosure. It represents a fourth-century fortified village that was in use during the Roman period. Finds here have included Roman pottery and coins which may be an indication that the occupants were on friendly terms with the Romans.

Stone hut sites are mainly found in Gwynedd and Dyfed. There are examples of circular and rectangular huts at Tŷ Mawr, Holyhead and Clynnog fawr.

When the Romans departed from Britain the invading Gwyddyl (Irish) chose Mona (Anglesey) as their main base and erected stone-walled fortresses to defend their captured territory. However, Caswallon Law hir (Long hand), the grandson of Cunedda Wledig, arrived on the scene to eject them. After numerous bloodthirsty battles he drove them from their stone fortresses. The survivors managed to retreat to Holy Island, but it was not long before Caswallon attacked their one remaining fortress and slew Seigi their chief near the entrance. Some of Seigi's followers managed to escape by taking to their boats, but all the other remaining Gwyddyl were killed. Seigi was honoured by the Welsh, who respected his bravery, and he was given a proper burial. In time he came to be regarded as a martyr and a chapel was erected on the location where he died. The present church (Capel Eglwys y Bedd – Church of the Grave) stands in the middle of Seigi's old fort at Llanbabo and there is an effigy of him holding a sword that can be seen in the niche of the doorway.

Cytiau'r Gwyddelod SH 214819 (114)

On Holy Island, Anglesey, the old habitations of the Irish are particularly numerous. There are a number on the side of Holyhead Mountain and many others by Porth Dofarch and Mynydd Celyn. The huts are circular in shape and about 15 feet to 20 feet in diameter and generally grouped together in small communities of between 12 to 50 huts. Sites were chosen in sheltered spots out of the prevailing winds and the entrances were on the south sides. Roofs would have been constructed with lengths of timber supporting layers of turf.

A large number of items have been found in these ancient houses, such as ornaments, stone lamps, necklaces, and bronze weapons, and it is likely that they were left in great haste when the army of Caswallon came over the horizon to massacre the Irish settlers.

Crannogs

Crannogs (lake dwellings) date from the Bronze Age and lasted well into the post-Roman period. They were defensive positions situated on artificial islands and were constructed of posts, rubble and earth. The word 'crannog' comes from the Irish – crann (a tree) – and these artificial islands are most common in Ireland and Scotland.

The Llangorse Canoe, Brecon Museum, Powys SO 129268 (161) – Grid reference of Bwlc

This dug-out canoe was discovered in 1925 in the mud at the bottom of the northern part of Llangorse Lake. Sir Cyril Fox, who made a study of it, said that 'It is not unreasonable to associate it with the island (Bwlc), wholly or in part artificial, which is situated in the same shore of the lake 500 yards away.'

The tiny island of Bwlc was first identified as a crannog in 1867 by E. N. Dumbleton, M.A.:

'Sailing by the island one day in 1867 I observed that the stones which stand out on the south and east side were strangely new looking, and most unlike the water-worn, rounded fragments that can be seen on the main shore that have been exposed to the action of the waves: neither did there seem to be any original rock basis at all. It was in fact nothing less than a huge heap of stones thrown into the water two or three feet in depth. Was this the key, I thought, to the old tradition of a city in the lake?'

Discoveries here included the piles on which was constructed a platform, which would have supported a few huts, numerous bones and some fragments of pottery. Nothing was found to give any idea of the period of occupation.

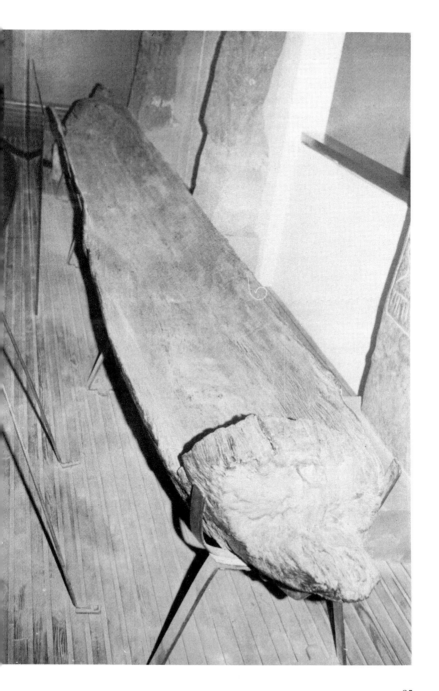

Llyn Llydaw, Gwynedd SH 5462 (115)

At the foot of Snowdon this beautiful mountain pool may possibly have once been the site of a lake dwelling. When the water level was lowered in 1862 an ancient canoe was exposed. It was of a very early design, known in Welsh as 'cafn unpren', and was fashioned from a single tree. This is the most primitive known form of boat.

Talley Lake, Dyfed SN 633 (146)

There is a tradition that a town lies beneath these waters, close to the remains of the fine old abbey. There are stories of towns buried beneath lakes throughout Wales and many parts of the world. Such traditions have been passed down since prehistoric times, when people dwelt in lake settlements and in caves for protection from the beasts of the forest as well as from human foes. It is possible that many of these folk tales are distant memories of lake dwellings and that Talley may once have been the site of a crannog, although there are no traces of one in present times.

Kenfig Pool, West Glamorgan SS 795815 (170)

This 70-acre pool has a circumference of two miles and is situated in a mass of sand dunes on the outskirts of Kenfig.

One of the old Charters of Margam Abbey describes an island and a building in ruins in the centre of the pool. If this was a crannog, it is no longer evident.

Carew Cross, Dyfed

5.
Celtic
Crosses

*'With the coming of Christianity the site of many
mark stones, "temples", and pagan altars became the
sites of Christian churches or churchyard crosses, and
almost all these, if of ancient foundation, align on the
straight tracks, as do crosses on the wayside.'*

Alfred Watkins, The Old Straight Track

A large number of ancient crosses were originally prehistoric standing stones (menhirs) which were converted into crosses by the addition of a Christian emblem chiselled upon them. One example is Carreg Bica on Maen Serth near Rhyader in Powys, where an unworked stone, standing about 7 feet high, has a cross incised in it. The finely decorated cross of Meiliog at Llowes church (Powys) is also believed to be an ancient menhir that has been reshaped (see page 79).

Crosses were often set up by wandering holy men before the erection of their simple church, and no doubt provided a gathering-point where preachers would speak.

'The setting up of a cross, "the truly precious rood", must precede the actual building of the church according to a decree of the Emperor Justinian A.D. 530.'

Johnson, Byways in
British Archaeology

Crosses in churchyards are usually to be found on the south side of the church; this may be associated with the traditional prejudice against burial on the north side.

Crosses were sometimes erected at crossroads and there have been instances recorded of suicides being buried at these locations. They were not allowed to be buried in churchyards, and crossroads were consequently the most sacred spots available: even though the person may have been denied a Christian burial there would at least be a cross near the grave.

Boundary crosses were sometimes erected to mark the limits of land owned by monasteries, and they often became regarded as assembly points.

It has been claimed that there are over four hundred variations of the basic shape of the cross. The most common is the Latin cross which has the transverse arm about a quarter of the way down the vertical line. †

The Greek cross has a horizontal line bisecting the vertical line. ✚

The Celtic cross has the arms enclosed in a circle. ⊕

The Maltese cross is shaped thus: ✠

The most typically Celtic form of cross is derived from the plain Latin cross. It is surrounded with a circular ring connecting the arms and making four circular hollows at the corners where the arms intersect.

In the ninth to tenth centuries carved stone crosses were beautifully ornamented with intricate patterns, which must have required a high degree of sculptural skill and endless patience. The finest examples of such Celtic religious sculpture can be seen at Carew, Nevern, Penally (Dyfed), Llantwit Major and Margam (West Glamorgan).

The Carew Cross displays interlaced decoration that is identical with many examples in Ireland, Scotland and the Isle of Man. It is also very similar to the cross at Nevern. It is of interest that the Carew Cross also serves as a memorial stone, bearing an eleventh-century inscription commemorating Margiteut, King of Dheubarth (south-west Wales) and great-grandson of Hywel Dda. (See pages 68 and 83)

Many ancient crosses were badly mutilated or destroyed completely in the seventeenth century when Parliament ordered, in 1641 and 1643, that all crosses should be pulled down. This destruction mainly took the form of breaking off the heads of the structures, leaving a mutilated shaft. In many instances they were reconstructed soon after 1643, and a very large number of churchyard crosses were restored in the nineteenth century.

Llanelieu Church, near Talgarth, Powys SO 185342 (161)

Near the entrance to this ancient church can be seen these two simple monumental stones inscribed with crosses and dots within a circle. Similar stones can be seen in other parts of Wales.

Glyndwyr's Dagger, Corwen Church, Clwyd SJ 078434 (125)

A stone forming a lintel over the priest's door is built into the church wall. It bears an incised cross which, according to legend, is the impression of Owain Glyndwyr's dagger that he hurled from the summit of a conical hill to the south of the church, overlooking Corwen. He threw it with such force that it made a deep indentation as it hit a stone in the vicinity of the church.

This cross was probably carved long before the time of Glyndwyr. The stone has been removed from its original location.

Capel Colman, near Boncath, off B4332, Dyfed SN 215383 (145)

This smooth and finely shaped stone was removed from its original position in the churchyard of Capel Colman at an unknown date to serve as a gatepost on a farm track. There is a local tradition that the stone was originally erected over the body of St Colman.

On the front of the stone is a cross of the same style and date as the one at Clydai church in a neighbouring parish. It shows an equal-armed cross in a circle. The rear of the stone is a central cross surmounted by a triangle, and there are also side strokes or curves. It has been suggested that this is intended to be a symbolic representation of the crucifixion on Mount Calvary, where three crosses were erected.

Llanveynoe Church, Olchon Valley, Black Mountains,
Herefordshire SO 303314 (161)

In this churchyard can be seen a plain short-armed cross of the type
frequently seen on Dartmoor. It is made from local sandstone and is of
Celtic origin. Standing 5 feet 6 inches high there is a groove 3 inches wide
and ¾ inch deep down the centre of the face. It may have been converted
into a water gutter after being removed at the time of the Reformation. It
was rediscovered in 1877 and replaced in the churchyard.

Llanrhidian, Gower, West Glamorgan SS 496923 (159)

On the common near Llanrhidian church is the remains of a Celtic cross that was at one time used as the village whipping-post. The pieces of iron embedded near the top and bottom of the stone were used to hold the unfortunate person firmly in position while receiving punishment.

Croes Faen, Near Tywyn (A493), Gwynedd SH 597014 (135)

In a corner of a field not far from the road is a slim stone, 7 feet 6 inches high, that is part of an ancient cross. According to a local tale, the district was at one time troubled by a flame-breathing dragon. The local people prayed every night at the cross until the dreadful beast disappeared.

Penmon Church, 4 miles north-east of Beaumaris, Anglesey SH 630807 (115) left

This impressive Celtic cross originally stood in a field 800 yards west of the church, but it has now been moved inside for safety. It has been dated at 1000 A.D. and is carved with faint patterns on all four sides. At the bottom of one face is a representation of a man with four animals – one of which appears to be lying on its back with its legs in the air.

Corwen Cross, Corwen Church (off A5) SJ 078434 (125)

Near the tower of Corwen Church stands this tall granite cross on an elliptical base about 12 inches thick. On the surface of the stone are seven depressions which, according to the Rev Elias Owen, 'strongly resemble the cup markings which are found occasionally on the capstones of cromlechs. They are arranged in an irregular manner and differ in size although similar in shape. They have been found in many different parts of the world and in some cases date from prehistoric times.'

It is certainly feasible that the base of this cross was once the capstone of a cromlech and many centuries ago removed from its original site and re-used for its present purpose.

St Teilo's Cross, Penally Church, near Tenby, Dyfed SS 117992 (158)

This slender stone cross is said to mark the birthplace of St Teilo. He was one of the early Bishops of Llandaff Cathedral (Cardiff) and was held in so much reverence that nearly twenty churches in Wales were dedicated to him.

When St Teilo died three churches insisted on receiving his body. To settle the dispute the body is said to have miraculously divided into three separate corpses. Consequently, each church had the honour of burying his remains, but the church of Llandaff has always claimed to contain the body of the real St Teilo.

Coychurch near Bridgend, West Glamorgan SS 939797 (170)

Inside this church is a very fine Celtic cross surmounting a tall shaft with interlaced decoration. It is the tallest stone cross in Glamorganshire (old county area).

At one time there was an inscription on the base of the cross but this has, unfortunately, been 'mislaid'. According to the Iolo manuscripts, this cross, when it stood in the churchyard, marked the burial place of St Crallo. Coychurch is the only church dedicated to this saint, who was the son of St Canna, to whom a church is dedicated at Llangan, a village two miles away (see page 79).

There is a replica of the Coychurch cross in the National Museum of Wales at Cardiff.

St Meulig's Cross, Llowes Church (A438), near Hay-on-Wye, Powys

In the Dark Ages this Celtic cross stood high on the Begwns to the north-west of Llowes. For an unknown reason it was removed and installed in this churchyard where it stood for about 800 years. In more recent times it was uprooted again and taken inside the church for safety.

The cross is 7 feet high, 3 feet wide and 10 inches thick. It has been suggested that it may originally have been a prehistoric standing stone that has been converted into a Christian cross. The plain cross on its one side dates back to the sixth or seventh century and the more intricately decorated cross on the other face (as in the illustration) was carved in the eleventh century.

St Meulig (Melig or Meiliog) was one of the many sons of Caw who, after serving as a soldier, became religious and studied under Cattwg at Llancarfan. Later, he settled in Llowes and built a small monastery. One of his more famous brothers was Gildas the historian. (See page 178)

The Dobitaucus Cross (also known as the Goblin Stone), St Roque's Chapel, near Merthyr Mawr, West Glamorgan SS 888781 (170)

On the highest point of Merthyr Mawr park, on private property, are the remains of an oratory known as St Roque's Chapel. Inside the derelict chapel are some ancient stone crosses which, for safety, were moved to this location from other places in the neighbourhood by Sir John Nicol in the late nineteenth century. The largest one is known as the Goblin Stone. It stood formerly in a field near the river. Standing 7 feet high, 3 feet wide and 18 inches thick, it apparently took six oxen to move it. The field in which it stood originally was said to be haunted by a ghost who, as soon as he caught any unlucky passerby, would force the person's hands through the openings of the cross and make him or her pray.

The Cross of Cynfelin,
Margam,
near Port Talbot,
West Glamorgan
SS 801863 (170)

Near Margam
churchyard is a
small museum that
houses a fascinating
collection of ancient
stones which have
been gathered together
from the local area and
preserved under one
roof.

The Conbelin (Cynfelin)
Cross is a beautiful example
of a ninth/tenth-century wheel
cross of local Pennant sandstone.
On the intricately decorated cross
is a Latin inscription in four
vertical lines.

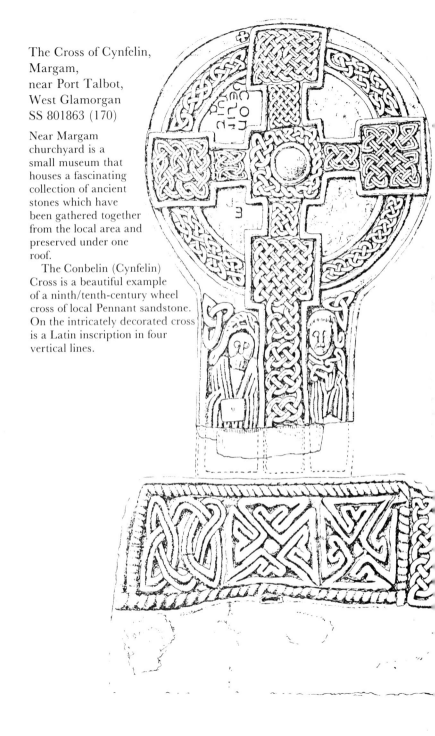

CONBELIN POSUIT HAN CRUCEM
Conbelin placed this cross

The two figures carved on this shaft are believed to be St John and the Blessed Virgin. The large block of stone forming the base of the cross is decorated with intertwining Celtic patterns on one side and human figures on the other (possibly a hunting scene).

This monument is rated as the finest disk cross to be seen in Wales and it resembles some of the sculptured stones of Scotland that depict hunting scenes.

Llangyfelach Churchyard, north-west of Swansea, West Glamorgan
SN 646989 (159)

In this churchyard can be seen a quadrangular cross base with a socket on its top that once supported a pillar cross. It is well decorated with a knotwork pattern and it is believed to date from the early ninth to tenth centuries.

The workmanship on this cross base is so fine that it is interesting to consider how beautiful the monument must have been when it was complete. Judging from the dimensions of the socket hole, the cross must have been no less than 8 or 10 feet high.

Crosses with socket bases are common in Ireland but quite rare in Wales. The other examples are to be seen at Penmon (page 77), Coychurch (page 78), and the wheel cross of Conbelin at Margam (page 78). The usual method of erecting a cross in pre-Norman times was to dig a hole in the ground, place the lower part of the shaft in the hole and fill in the earth around it.

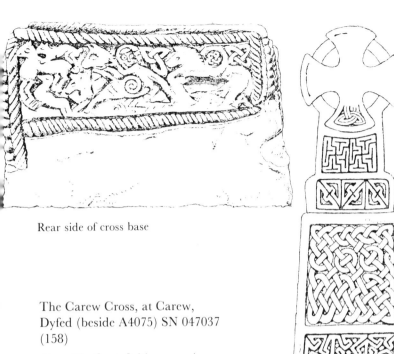

Rear side of cross base

The Carew Cross, at Carew,
Dyfed (beside A4075) SN 047037
(158)

One of the finest Celtic crosses in
Britain, the Carew Cross probably
dates from the eleventh century. It
may be described as a wheel-headed
cross on a tall shaft which is
beautifully inscribed with intricate
patterns. It also serves as a memorial
stone, for on the reverse side is an
inscription commemorating
Margiteut (Maredydd ap Ewin) who
became King of Dheubarth (south-
west Wales) in 1033 A.D.. He was a
great-grandson of Hywel Dda (the
Good) and was killed in a battle in
1035 A.D. when Cynan ap Seisyllt
invaded Dyfed and Dheubarth. This
cross was erected as a royal memorial
soon after that date.

*'A single false step, a slip of the tool, and
the entire cross would have been ruined.
But we do not find false cuts. The whole is
of almost mechanical perfection, and must
have been the result of endless practice.'*

Nora Chadwick, The Celts

The Llanynis Pillar Cross, Brecon Museum, Powys

This well-decorated stone cross is a beautiful piece of workmanship, probably dating from the ninth century.

Llangan, 4 miles east of Bridgend, West Glamorgan SS 957777 (170)

This ancient church is dedicated to St Canna, wife of St Sadwrn. In the churchyard is a Celtic wheel cross carved with a crude representation of the crucifixion showing a soldier piercing the side of Christ and a 'sponge bearer' standing on the other side. It is believed to have been carved in the ninth century.

St Canna was mother of St Crallo whose church was a few miles away at Coychurch – where the Cross of St Crallo can be seen. (See page 78)

Llanveynoe Church, Olchon Valley, Black Mountains, on the border of Wales, Herefordshire SO 303314 (161)

This primitive crucifixion stone is in a church just outside Wales, but it has been included because it is of particular interest – and Llanveynoe used to be in Wales anyway!

The body on the cross appears to be wearing a tunic and the feet are positioned as if he is standing. The arms are straight and the head leans slightly to one side. The presence of some cup marks on the slab may indicate that this is a Christianized pagan stone.

Bosherton Churchyard, south of Pembroke, Dyfed SN 966948 (158)

This unusual preaching cross with a vague face carved on it stands on a two-tiered base. The cross has been placed on a locally hewn upright and was once part of a stone crucifix, predating the upright by many centuries.

Sundial Stone, Clynnog fawr, A499, south-west of Caernarvon, Gwynedd SH 414497 (115)

This is not a Celtic cross but an ancient carved sundial of Anglo-Saxon design. Such stones as these are common in Ireland and usually date from the seventh or eighth century. The top of the stone has not been sliced off – only the lower half of the circle is necessary, for the shadow cast from a pointer placed in the central hole would be cast downwards. The semicircle is divided into four equal parts by lines radiating from the centre. It is a unique stone in Wales and is certainly pre-Norman. It was scheduled as an ancient monument in 1950.

The sundial is the oldest method of telling the time in the world; it is mentioned in the Old Testament and was commonly used by the Egyptians.

6.
Memorial Stones
of the Dark Ages

*'To be ignorant of what happened before you were
born is to be forever a child. For what is man's
lifetime unless the memory of past events is woven
with those of earlier times.'*

Cicero

The period of history between the departure of the Romans and the coming of the Normans has popularly become known as the Dark Ages, for the historical records of these times are virtually non-existent and there is a general lack of datable discoveries of this period. However, about four hundred inscribed and decorated memorial stones attributed to the fifth to seventh and the ninth to eleventh centuries have been located and are still available for study, although unfortunately few of them remain on their original sites.

Many of the fifth- and sixth-century memorial stones were originally sited beside the roads leading to the Roman forts – no doubt a copy of the Roman custom of setting up tombstones beside their highways. When the Romans were withdrawn from Britain by Magnus Maximus in 383 A.D., Wales became fragmented into petty kingdoms of varying size and power, each ruled by a king or prince. Many of the Roman fashions were retained and the erection of inscribed memorial stones was one of them.

These Dark Age memorial stones are very important, for they provide contemporary records of the conversion of Wales to Christianity and the development of the Celtic church. The stones were often decorated with a cross or some other Christian symbol, which was either incised or cut in low relief to show that the deceased was a Christian.

The inscribed stones were sometimes set up in conspicuous places as memorials and in some instances were erected on small earthworks, which suggests that they were sites of grave mounds. (For example, the original site of the Bodvoc Stone on Margam Mountain. See page 45) This was not always the case, however; sometimes the inscribed stones were set up in isolation and did not mark the actual burial site. Excavation of Maen Madoc, near Ystradfellte (Powys), has shown quite conclusively that there was no burial beside the stone of Dervacus, on the side of the Sarn Helen running across the moor of Fforest Fawr to the Roman fort at Coelbren.

Maen y Morynion (The Maiden's Stone), Brecon Museum, Powys

This large stone used to stand on the side of a Roman road to the west of
Brecon. Although badly eroded by the elements it still shows clearly the
figures of a Roman soldier and his wife. There used to be a legible
inscription on the stone which read:
ALANCIA CIVIS ET CONJUNX EJUS HIC EST – Alancia the citizen
and his wife are here buried.

The stone was discovered in 1698 during excavations for the construction
of a barn near Gaer Farm, which adjoins Gaer Bannium, and was then
removed to the position shown in the illustration, near the Roman road.

In some cases the inscribed stones were buried inside the graves. The stone of Brochmael and his wife Caune formed the cover stone to a cist containing a 6 foot skeleton, found in a cemetery of forty graves near Pentrefoelas (Clwyd). The Domnic stone found at Llangwyryfon was also found buried in the grave.

To merit a memorial stone the deceased had to be a person of some importance (king, prince, bishop or saint) and the body was generally laid in a long cist of rough slabs and orientated east-to-west in accordance with Christian belief.

In Wales there are fifty-five inscribed stones that bear Ogham inscriptions and twenty-six of them are bilingual, for the Ogham epitaph is accompanied by a duplicate inscription in Latin capitals. Ogham is an early system of writing that was developed in Ireland and consists of a series of notches and strokes incised along the edges of stones. Such stones are found in large numbers in Ireland and about two hundred have been discovered in the counties of Kerry, Cork and Waterford.

It was Edward Llwyd who, in 1693, first commented on the Ogham marks which he noticed on a drawing of the Pool Park stone (which formerly stood on Bryn y Beddau near Clocaenug), although he had no idea of their purpose. '. . . as far as ye strokes on ye edges, I met with them on other tombstones and I make not ye least question but this is also a tombstone.' In 1846, Professor Westwood recognized the marks on the edges of a stone at Kenfig (West Glamorgan) as Oghams, but it was not until a meeting of the Cambrian Archaeological Association, when details of the St Dogmael's Stone Oghams were discussed, that the Welsh inscriptions of Ogham were seriously and systematically researched.

Ogham stones are more common in parts of Wales that are closer to Ireland. During the fifth and sixth centuries the churches of Wales and Ireland were closely linked and it is possible that some of the Irish holy men may have erected the Ogham stones in Wales. It is of interest that in Ireland there are no Ogham stones that bear Latin inscriptions as well.

In the sixth century the language of Goidelic was much used in South Wales, although Latin was obviously the literary language in general use, for when the Romans withdrew from Wales the Britons continued to use Roman lettering and Latin names when inscribing their memorial stones. It must be remembered that the ancient songs, tales and sayings of the bards were handed down orally and any knowledge of letters and writing had been obtained from the Romans, for the Celts had no native alphabet or means of writing.

Ogma was the Gaelic god of literature and eloquence who married Eton, the daughter of Diancecht, the god of medicine. So, as patron of literature, Ogma was naturally credited with being the inventor of the Ogham alphabet. (See page 103 for further details.)

Locations of Ogham stones in Wales (in the old counties):

Pembrokeshire	28
Cardiganshire	8
Denbighshire	3
Caernarvonshire	14
Flintshire	1
Montgomeryshire	1
Breconshire	4
Glamorganshire	2
Carmarthenshire	6

No Ogham stones have been found on Anglesey.

By 600 A.D. it seems that Ogham script was no longer in use in Wales, but the custom of setting up inscribed tombstones with Latin inscriptions and Celtic decorations lasted until the end of the eleventh century. The inscriptions on many of the stones were written in bad Latin, showing that composition in that language was in decline.

By 1853 a large proportion of the most important of the remaining inscribed stones of Wales had been discovered and recorded, although from time to time a new one comes to light. Unfortunately, many hundreds of important stones must have been destroyed over the centuries and broken up for road building and house construction. One of the later inscribed stones to be discovered was found in St David's Cathedral in 1891. It is a memorial to Hedd and Isacc, sons of Bishop Abraham who presided there from 1078 to 1080.

'Time which antiquates Antiquities, and hath an art to make dust of all things, hath yet spared these minor monuments.'

Sir Thomas Browne, Urne-buriall

The Corbalengi Stone, off A487 between Cardigan and Newquay, Dyfed SN 288514 (145)

This ancient stone stands in the middle of a field, half a mile from Penbryn church. It stands about 5 feet high and bears the inscription COR BALENGI JUCIT ORDOUS which translates as 'The heart of Balencus, the Ordovician lies here.' He was probably a Welshman with a Roman name. The Ordovician territory was in mid-Wales.

When the Rev Henry Jenkins excavated the mound beneath the stone in 1850, he discovered an urn containing ashes, coins of silver and bronze, and a gold chain of the reign of the Roman Emperor Vespasian. Later excavations revealed a quantity of burnt bones and remains of weapons. It is interesting that there is a local legend of fourteen Roman ships landing at Tresaith and setting up camp on the spot where the stone stands. Perhaps the local people fought a battle here against the invading Romans.

Carreg Faen Hir, Gelligaer Common, below Carn y Bugail, north of Bedlinog, Mid Glamorgan SO 104034 (171)

This ancient stone stands on the side of the Sarn Helen, where it crosses Cefn Gelligaer one mile south of Fochriw. Sloping at a crazy angle, the slim stone is 8 feet 6 inches high by 1 foot 6 inches wide. There used to be an inscription on the eastern face but this is unfortunately no longer visible. However, it once read DEFROIHI and it has been suggested that this could be a reference to St Dubricius (Dyfrig).

The inscription was defaced by a party of colliers from the Dowlais works who came here one afternoon about eighty years ago and vandalized the inscription by chipping it away with hammers.

Treasure is said to be buried beneath the stone and some local farmers in the nineteenth century tried to uproot it – this is probably why it leans – but a violent thunderstorm drove them away.

The Stone of Doctor Melus, St Cian's Church, Llangian, Abersoch,
Gwynedd SH 295289 (123)

On the south side of the churchyard is a very unusual sixth-century
inscribed stone, with lettering in three vertical lines which reads:

MELI MEDICI	(the stone of) the Doctor Melus
MELI MARTINI	Son of Martinus
JACIT	He lies (here)

It is rare for an inscribed stone in Wales to refer to the dead man's
profession so this memorial stone is of special interest.

Llangian church is believed to have been founded by Peris in conjunction
with Cian, his servant, but it was Cian who probably spent more time
here. These two saints are referred to in the Black Book of Carmarthen,
and in the poetry of Aneirin and Taliesin.

St Sadwrn's Stone, Llansadwrn Church, Anglesey, Gwynedd SH 554758 (115)

Inside the church is the tombstone of St Sadwrn the founder. It was found under the wall of the chancel and it bears the inscription:

HIC BEATU (S) SATURNINUS SE (PULTIS I) ACIT.
ET SUA SA (NCTA) CONIUX P(AX).
Here lies buried blessed . . . Saturninus and his saintly wife
Peace be with you both.

Sadwrn was an Armorican prince (from Brittany) and the brother of St Illtud, the founder of the great college at Llantwit Major in South Glamorgan (see page 155). Sadwrn's wife was Canna, his cousin. After his death she remarried and became the mother of Elian the pilgrim.

A few miles away at Beaumaris is a tomb, the sides of which are decorated with delicately carved representations of Anglesey saints. Two of them show Sadwrn and Canna. He is depicted wearing armour. His sword is in a sheath and he holds a pilgrim's staff in his left hand and appears to be giving a benediction with his right hand.

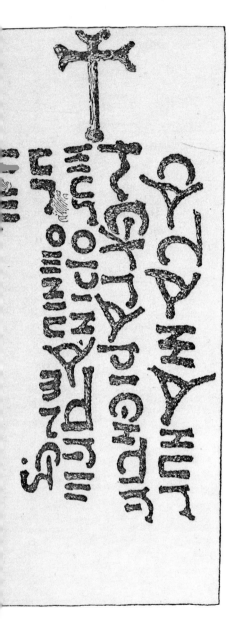

The Cadfan Stone, Llangadwaladr Church, Aberffraw, Anglesey SH 383693 (114)

Set into the north wall of the chancel is this ancient stone inscribed in Latin. It commemorates Cadfan who was a seventh-century king of Gwynedd.

CATAMANUS REX SAPIENTISIMUS OPINATISIMUS, OMNIUM REGUM

This translates as 'Cadfan the king, wisest and most splendid of all kings.'

Cadfan died in 625 A.D. and was succeeded by his son Cadwallon, who was killed in a battle in 634 A.D. near Hexham against King Oswald of Northumbria. His grandson, Cadwaladr, then ruled until 664 A.D., when according to the Welsh Chronicle, 'the crown of the Isle of Britain came to an end': a terrible plague broke out, spreading death and desolation over Britain and Ireland. Cadwaladr fell victim to it and was buried in this church which bears his name. He is depicted in one of the stained glass windows.

Kenyric's Stone, St Illtud's Church, Llanelltyd, near Harlech,
Gwynedd SH 717195 (124)

Inside this ancient church is a stone, resembling a coffin lid, which was
found in 1876 among debris in an outbuilding near the church. A Latin
inscription reads:

VESTIGUM KENRIC TENETURE IN CAPITRE
LAPIDID ET IPESEMET ANTEQUOM
PEREGRE PRAFECTUS EST.

– The footprint of Kenyric (Cynwrig) imprinted at the head of this stone
before he set out for foreign parts.

A vague footprint can be seen on the stone. The question is whether his
journey was to the far off land of Jerusalem or merely to the island of
Bardsey. Kenyric may have had the imprint of his foot carved on the stone
to 'guarantee' a safe return from his travels.

The Bodvocus Stone, Margam Museum, near Port Talbot, West Glamorgan SS 801863 (170)

Previously known as Maen y Dythyrog (Lettered Stone), this memorial stone used to stand on a bare hilltop about two miles from Margam Abbey. It is about 4 feet high by 12 inches wide and 7 inches thick. The Latin inscription in four vertical lines reads:

BODVOC – HIC IACIT/FILIUS CATOTIGIRNI/PRONEPVS ETERNALI(S)/VEDOMAV – (The stone) of Bodvoc. Here he lies, son of Catotigirnus (and) great grandson of Eternalis Vedomavus.

A local belief warns that whoever reads the inscription on the stone dies within the year.

The following quotation was once relevant to the original site of the stone:

'It stands alone on the hill and whistles to the future ages the name of Bodvocus, the shaggy grass waves to the wind.'

David Lloyd Isaac, *Silvriana*

St Tyddud's Church, Penmachno, near Bettws y Coed, Gwynedd SH 790505 (115)

Four inscribed stones dating from the sixth century can be seen inside this church. Of special interest is the Magistrati stone which was brought here from Beddau Gwyr Ardudwy near a Roman road in the parish of Ffestiniog. It bears a Latin inscription in five lines:

CANTIORIX HIC JACIT / VENEDOTIS CIVES FVIT /
CONSOBRINOS / MAGLI / MAGISTRAT

This translates as: 'Cantiorix lies here. He was a citizen of Venedos (and) cousin of Maglos the Magistrate.'

This is the only known instance of the use of the word magistrate on an inscribed stone of this period.

Bedd Porius, south of Trawsfynydd, on moorland above A487, Gwynedd SH 734316 (124)

About one mile south of Llyn Gelli Gain near Rhiw Goch is an inscribed stone (fifth to sixth century) that marks the grave of Porius. It is, in fact, only a replica, for the original stone is now kept in the National Museum at Cardiff. The grave is enclosed by railings and the inscription reads:

PORIUS HIC IN TUMULO JACET HOMO PLANUS FUIT – Here in this grave lies Porius. He was a plain man.

Alternatively: Porius lies here in this tomb. He was a leper.

99

The Cadfan Stone, St Cadfan's Church, Tywyn, Gwynedd SN 587009 (135)

At one time this inscribed stone used to stand in the churchyard within four upright stones that enclosed a quadrangular space where no burials were made. The inscription is in archaic Welsh (probably one of the earliest records of the Welsh language) and it records that this was the burial site of St Cadfan and that his great patron St Cyngen, Prince of Powys and this area of land, lies beside him:

*'Beneath the mound of Cynfael lies Cadfan
Where the earth extols his praise, let him
rest without a blemish.
The body of Cyngen and between them will
be the marks.'*

Cadfan was the son of Eneos Lydewig by Gwenteirbran, a daughter of Emyr Llydaw, a prince of Armorica. In the sixth century Cadfan came to Wales and founded the churches of Tywyn and Llangadfan (Powys).

Cyngen was the son of Cadell and a contemporary of Cadfan (during the period 500–542 A.D.). He succeeded his father in the principality of Powys and was distinguished for his patronage to the saints and liberal endowments to the church. His son was Brochwel ysgythrog. (see page 128).

In 1761 this stone was found to be in use as a gatepost but, fortunately, someone recognized it as an object of historical importance and it has been preserved.

The Catacus Stone, Llanvihangel Cwmdu, north of Crickhowell, A479, Powys SO 181238 (161)

This late sixth-century memorial stone is built into a buttress on the south side of the church. It is 5 feet 4 inches high and 22 inches wide and bears a Latin inscription in two lines reading vertically:

CATACUS HIC IACIT/ FILIUS TEGERNACUS.
Catacus lies here, son (of) Tegernacus.

It might be supposed that here we have the memorial of Cattwg Ddoeth (Cattwg the Wise, son of Gwynlliw), the founder of many churches in Glamorgan, Gwent and Breconshire, including the one at Llangattock close to Crickhowell and not far from Cwmdu. But he was the son of Gwynlliw and not Tegernacus. Yet is it not a strange coincidence that the stone previously stood in a field called Tir Gwenlli, about a mile south west of the church, and that this valley was once known as Cwm Cattwg?

The name of Catuc also appeared on a stone which once stood at the threshold of Llandefailog fach church (see page 106) but this was unfortunately either destroyed or lost. It may also be observed that Tegernacus may be identical to Tegernacus the son of Martius, whose memorial stone was found at Capel Brithdir (see page 102).

The Tegernacus Stone, National Museum, Cardiff, South Glamorgan

Here can be seen a seventh-century pillar stone, about 9 feet high, that used to stand on the Cefn y Brithdir ridge near Tirphil (Mid Glamorgan) beside an ancient track. The inscription TEGERNACUS FILIUS MARTI HIC IACIT in four lines reading vertically downwards may be translated as: Tegernacus son of Martius lies here.

It is of interest that the name Tegernacus also appears on the Cwmdu stone (see page 101) where it refers to Catacus the son of Tegernacus – an example of how some of these memorial stones interrelate.

Tegernacus (Tegerna) was the son of Madrun, the daughter of Vortigern, which makes this stone of particular importance, for it may well be the memorial stone of Vortigern's grandson.

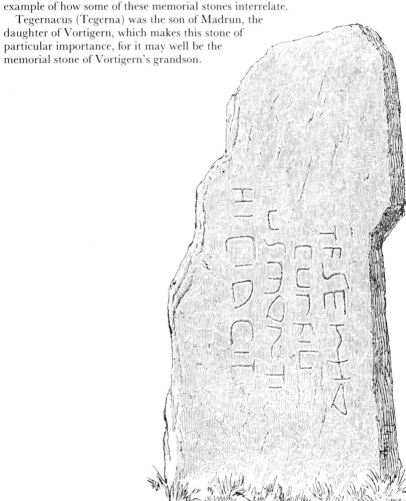

Ogham Writing

This script was invented in south-west Ireland in the fourth century. The twenty letters of the Latin alphabet are represented by notches (the vowels) and strokes (the consonants). The vowels are notched along the line and the consonantal strokes – single, double, treble, quadruple and quintuple – were either cut across the line or to one side of it. Generally, the edge of the stone provided the central line.

An early Irish manuscript tells of secret messages being sent by the exchange of sticks bearing cuts which were passed between important people. It would appear that Ogham writing was used by a few Irish people right up until the nineteenth century: a story is told of an Irish farmer who was being prosecuted for not having his name on his cart; the man protested that he had done this and managed to prove it. He had carved his name on the cart in Ogham and the case failed.

The key to the Ogham alphabet is given in the book of Ballymote, a compilation of the fourteenth century preserved in the Royal Irish Academy in Dublin. It is interesting that a knowledge of the Ogham letters survived among Irish country people in a rhyme beginning with the following lines:

> *For B one stroke at your right hand,*
> *And L doth always two dessent,*
> *For F draw three, for S make four,*
> *When you want N you add one more.*

The Ogham Alphabet

I	C
E	T
U	D
O A	H
Z	N
N and G	S
G	F
M	L
Q	B

Ogham Stone, Caldey Island, near Tenby, Dyfed SS 141962 (152)

Inside the ancient church of St Illtud on the island of Caldey is this sixth-century stone which bears the remnants of an Ogham inscription on both edges of the face and, originally, probably across the top as well. It reads upwards on the left edge and downwards on the right.

(The stone) of Magl . . . Dubr . . .

It is feasible that this refers to the servant of Dubricius – meaning Piro.

In about 750 A.D. a cross and the following Latin inscription were added to the old Ogham epitaph:

'And I have marked it with the sign of the cross, I beseech all that pass hereby to pray for the soul of Catuocanus.' (Possibly a reference to Cadwgan.)

The stone was discovered in the ruins of the priory in the nineteenth century. For a while it became the lintel of a window, and then a garden seat, before its importance was recognized and it was taken inside the priory church for safety.

The Turpili Stone, Brecon Museum, Powys

This rough pillar stone was discovered on the farm of Tyr yn y Wlad near Crickhowell and for a while it served as a footbridge in Glanusk Park. It bears Ogham and Latin inscriptions:

The Ogham reads TURPILI (LI MAQUI TRIL) LUNI
(The Stone) of Turpillius (son) of Trillunus.
In Latin it reads TVRPILLI (h) 'ICIA/CIT/PVVERI TRILVNI DVNOCA/TI.
(The Stone) of Turpillius. He lies here, son of Trilunus Dunocatus.

The name Dunocati becomes Dincat in the *Liber Landavensis*.

The Cross of Brimail, Llandefaelog fach, 3
miles north of Brecon, Powys SN 034324
(160)

Here can be seen a tall, narrow Celtic cross slab
which formerly stood in the churchyard but has
now been taken inside the church for safety. These
stones are common in Ireland and the Isle of
Man but rare in Wales.

It depicts a male figure wearing a long tunic,
holding a spear across his right shoulder with his
right hand and a dagger in his left hand. The
inscription in two lines reading horizontally is
BRIAMAIL/FLOU – (The Cross of) Briamail
Flou.

It is recorded that there used to be a stone at
this church inscribed CATVC, but this has
unfortunately been lost. It may well have
been a memorial stone to St Cattwg and
would have been of considerable importance.
It is a mystery why Cattwg should be
connected with this parish. The stone in
question was described by Theophilus Jones
in 1890, but it has since disappeared.

Rhun, the son of Brychan, is reputed to be
buried here, and the church is dedicated to
St Tyfailog, a corruption of Maelog, who
was the youngest son of Caw and a brother
of St Gildas. The present name is probably a
corruption of Llanmaelog. (See page 79 for a
description of St Maelog's Cross at Lowes
Church, Powys.)

There are many other instances of
important memorial stones that have now
disappeared. For example, there used to be a
stone standing on a tumulus known as Caer
Saint, near the old Roman fort of Segentium
at Caernarvon (Gwynedd). It was inscribed
with the names of Constantine (the Great)
and his father Magnus Maximus.

2.

The Cross-slab of Moridic from Llanhamlach Church, near Brecon, Powys. (Now at Brecon Museum)

This interesting stone, which combines a cross with figures on either side, is obviously intended to depict the Crucifixion scene. The figure on the left appears to be holding a book in his right hand while the man on the right is shown in an attitude of prayer. He has both hands raised – the ancient attitude of prayer as seen in the painting of the Oranti and Daniel in the Den of Lions in the Catacombs of Rome.

One of the figures has a circle with a central dot on each side of the head just above the shoulders, and a circle with three rays issuing from below on each of the breasts.

An inscription on the side of the stone translates as 'Moridic set up this stone', which is an indication that it was once planted upright in the ground.

Erect Cross-slab of Moridic at Llanhamlach.

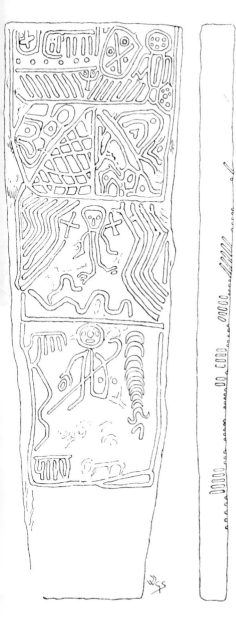

The Llywel Stone, Brecon Museum, Powys

The picture shows a cast replica of a sixth-century decorated and inscribed stone, found near Trecastle to the west of Brecon. The original is now in the British Museum, London. It is elaborately carved with symbols and human figures and bears an inscription in Ogham and Latin: in Ogham it reads MAQUTRENI SALICIDUNI which translates as (The stone) of Maqutrenus Salicidunus. The Latin version is MACCUTRENI + SALICIDVNI which means (The stone) of Maccutrenus Salicidunus.

The decoration on the stone is unique among the early Christian memorial stones of Wales, and it may convey a message in its strange symbols and designs that, so far, have not been deciphered.

Llanrhidian Church, Gower, West Glamorgan SS 496923 (159)

A large limestone block of great antiquity, known as the Leper Stone, can be seen inside the porch of this church. It is decorated with crude representations of animal and human figures and was found many years ago, buried near the tower, and was subsequently transferred to the church porch.

Sacred Monograms

In the early days of the Christian Church groups of letters derived from Greek and Latin words were used as symbols of Christ. The earliest examples of these can be seen in the Catacombs of Rome and have been dated 331 A.D.

The Chi Rho monogram is derived from the first two letters of XPICTOC, a Greek word meaning Christ, and it preceded the cross as a common symbol of Christ. It originated in 312 A.D. when the Emperor Constantine gained a great victory over his rival

Maxentius. Writings by Lacentius record that on the eve of the encounter:

'Constantine was admonished in a dream to paint on his soldiers' shields the heavenly sign of God, and so to give battle. He does so as he is commanded, and with the letter X placed transversely, having one bent extremity bent round, he marks their shields with Christus. Armed with this sign his army draws the sword.'

The next day, after conquering under the sign of the cross, Constantine entered Rome in triumph and summoning artists commanded them to make the standard of which Eusebius gives the following description:

'It was a long spear, gilt and provided with a transverse bar like a cross. Above, at the top of this same spear, was fixed a wreath of gold and precious stones. In the centre of the wreath was the sign of the saving name (of Jesus Christ); that is to say a monogram setting forth this holy name by its first two letters combined, the P in the middle of the X. These same letters the Emperor was accustomed henceforth to wear on his helmet.'

The use of the Chi Rho monogram of Christ soon spread from Rome to other countries and it may be found on numerous monuments in France which are dated between the years 340 and 377 A.D.

In Wales, one may find the Chi Rho monogram on several inscribed stones and crosses, the Carausius stone at Penmachno being a good example.

The first and last letters of the Greek alphabet (Alpha and Omega) were sometimes used to denote the eternity and infinity of God and were often used in conjunction with another symbol such as the cross:

'The lord said "I am alpha and omega, the beginning and the ending."'

Rev 1:8

The circle was also regarded as a symbol of eternity because it is without beginning or end.

Another example of the XPS symbol can be seen on the stone of St Gwnws near Ystrad Meurig (see page 112). The alpha and omega symbols can be seen on a small cross-slab at St Edren's church in Dyfed.

The Carausius Stone, Penmachno Church, Gwynedd SH 790505 (115)

This stone is inscribed with the Chi Rho monogram, giving evidence that it marked the site of a Christian burial. The translation of the inscription is:

CARAUSIUS lies here in this mound of stones.

St Gwnws's Church, Llanwnws, Ystwyth Valley, near Tyn y graig, Dyfed SN 684695 (135)

Inside this church is a rough pillar stone bearing a Latin ring cross and the letters XPS, which is the Greek contraction for 'Christus'. It also displays a Latin inscription in twelve lines, reading horizontally, which may be translated as follows:

'Whosoever may decipher this name, let him utter a benediction on the spirit of Hirodil – son of Carotinn.'

It is quite possible that this is the memorial stone of Hywel Dda ('The Great'), son of Catell, who died in 950 A.D. (see page 126). This would make the stone of considerable importance.

7.
Dark Age Dominions

'Remember the days of old
Consider the days of many generations
Enquire, I pray thee, of the former ages;
Prepare thyself to the search of their fathers
For we are but as yesterday.'

Owen Morgan

In the Dark Ages Wales was divided up into small independent kingdoms which were ruled by separate dynasties. The five greater kingdoms were Gwynedd, Powys, Dehubarth and Morgannwg, and these areas contained numerous sub-kingdoms such as Buellt, Ystrad Tywi, Rhufoniog, Cyweli, Gwyr and Brycheiniog – where sons and grandsons of the rulers were appointed as 'area kings'.

Vortigern of Vortigerninia

Cwm Gwytheyrn (Vortigern's Valley) on the west side of Yr Eifl on the Lleyn Peninsula, Gwynedd SH 350452 (123)

This deep valley near the bay of Porth y Nant is associated with the last days of King Gwrtheyrn, otherwise known as Vortigern (in Latin, Victorius or Victorinius). He was a Romano-Briton, the son of Vitalis, the son of Vitalianus. From the inscribed pillar of Eliseg (see page 124) we can ascertain that Vortigern married Severa, the daughter of Maximus by whom he had a son named Brydw, who was blessed by St Germanus (Garmon).

There are accounts of Vortigern operating in the mountains of Snowdonia, mid-Wales and in south-west Wales. Gwrtheyrnion (Vortigerninia) was the little kingdom centred on the Rhyader area where he ruled, which later became known as Radnorshire. His descendants ruled over Powys.

In 449 A.D. Vortigern invited the Jutes to assist the Britons against the Picts and the Scots, and he is referred to in the Welsh Triads as 'one of the three drunkards of the Isle of Britain, who when intoxicated gave up the Isle of Thanet to Hengist'.

The story goes that Vortigern was enamoured with the beauty of Rowena, the daughter of Hengist the Saxon, and while intoxicated with wine and ale, he demanded her for a wife, promising her father to give him anything in return that he asked for. Hengist, after consultation with his followers, demanded the province known as Ceint or Kentland.

In the battles that subsequently followed with the Saxons, Vortigern's son Vortimer fought bravely against the invaders, but, wounded in battle and poisoned by Rowena, he died.

Meanwhile Vortigern, discredited and deposed, with most of the Britons in revolt against him under Aurelius Ambrosius, fled to his castle in Gwrtheyrnion where he was besieged and had to head further north. His last stronghold is said to be in numerous places, including Carreg

Gwrtheyrn on the Teifi near Llandyssul in Dyfed. However, Cwm Gwytheyrn on the Lleyn Peninsula in Gwynedd has a much stronger claim for the site of Vortigern's last stand. He is supposed to have retreated to this deep valley and built a wooden castle, which was dramatically struck by lightning and set on fire. In the castle at the time was Madryn, wife of Ynyr, King of Gwent, with her small son. She fled from the blazing fortress and made her way to a fortified hilltop which now bears her name – Carn Fadryn. She later sailed from North Wales and went to live in Cornwall.

A large tumulus known as Bedd Gwrtheyrn on the eastern side of the valley was excavated in the nineteenth century: a large skeleton was discovered in a stone coffin and was claimed to be the remains of King Vortigern. One version of the story says that he perished inside his burning castle; alternatively, he is supposed to have committed suicide by jumping off Carreg y Llam (The Rock of the Leap) into the sea.

Vortigern's granddaughter was Madrun, who founded a school at Trawsfynydd; her name is also remembered at Garth Madrun, known as Talgarth, which became the main court of Brychan Brycheiniog (see page 130).

Vitalianus Stone, Nevern Church, Dyfed SN 083401 (145)

Vortigern's son, Vortimer, was known as Vitalianus, and it is feasible that it is his memorial stone that can be seen here at the church of St Brynach. It stands to the east of the porch and bears inscriptions both in Ogham and Latin:

Ogham: VITALIANI (The stone of) Vitalianus
Latin: VITALIANI EMERETO (The stone of) Vitalianus

Maelgwyn of Gwynedd

Maelgwyn Gwynedd was descended from Cunedda Wledig, a fifth-century Romano-British chieftain who, with his eight sons, drove the Venedotae from north-west Wales back to Ireland. The sons of Cunedda were allocated various parts of Wales to govern and their names subsequently became associated with those particular areas.

Ceredig ruled Ceredigion (Cardigan)
Arwystl ruled Arwysti (part of Montgomeryshire)
Dunod ruled Dunodig (parts of Merionethshire and Caernarvonshire)
Edeyrn ruled Edeyrnion (part of Merionethshire)
Rhuvan ruled Rhuvoniog (part of Caernarvonshire and Denbighshire)
Meirion ruled Meirion (part of Meirionethshire)
Coel and Dogfael ruled Coeleian and Dogvellin (Denbighshire)

The grandson of Cunedda Wledig was Caswallon Lawhir, who chased the Irish out of North Wales, and his son was Maelgwyn Gwynedd.

Deganwy Castle, south of Llandudno, overlooking the mouth of the Conwy SH 783795 (115)

Din-gonwy means the castle on the Conwy. In the middle of the sixth century it was the headquarters of Maelgwyn Gwynedd, who established his citadel on a knoll near the mouth of the river, where twin hills rise to a height of 350 feet, making it an ideal site for a fortress. The area of land just below the castle hill is called Maesdu (Black Meadow), where many a bloody battle must have taken place.

Maelgwyn Gwynedd was the son of Caswallon Lawhir (Long Hand) who overthrew the Goidels of North Wales (see page 63) and he was referred to by Gildas as the 'Dragon of the Island'. Maelgwyn was a tall and powerful man who was often referred to as Maelgwyn Hir ('the Tall'). He had an evil reputation and accomplished many dirty deeds. It is said that he overthrew his uncle to take his crown, then murdered his wife, the sister of Brochwel Ysgythrog (King of Powys), and killed a nephew to marry this faithless spouse.

His stronghold at Deganwy was probably constructed in timber, and it suffered a long history of misfortunes. It was burnt by lightning in 860 A.D., rebuilt by Robert of Rhuddlan, captured and recaptured and then finally demolished, when King Edward I built Conwy Castle on the opposite side of the river. The stones from Deganwy were then taken by

boat across the river to be used in the construction of Conwy's town walls. Only a few fragments of the stone castle now remain.

Maelgwyn's name is preserved in this area in local features such as Bryn Maelgwyn (Maelgwyn's Hill) near Deganwy and Traeth Maelgwyn (Maelgwyn's Strand) near Borth.

Traeth Maelgwyn, north of Borth at the mouth of the Afon Dyfi, Gwynedd SN 6293 (135)

This large expanse of sand at Traeth Maelgwyn was once the legendary scene of a curious competition which bears some similarity to the story of King Canute. The event took place after Maelgwyn had murdered his uncle and was anxious to become king in his place. He summoned the important Welsh chieftains of the area to meet him at this stretch of sand near Ynyslas. They were asked to sit in chairs on the sand as the tide swept up the Dyfi, and it was agreed that the man who dared to remain the longest in his chair would be recognized as king by all those present.

Crafty Maelgwyn had arranged for a special chair to be prepared – fitted with waxed birds' wings which would float in the water; so as the rising tide compelled all the other men to leave their chairs, Maelgwyn remained seated on his floating chair and won the contest.

There are numerous tales of quarrels that Maelgwyn had with the church, and in particular some of the 'saints' who were active in that area. On one occasion Maelgwyn discovered that Padarn, the Bishop of

118

Llanbadarn near Aberystwyth, had a secret store of treasure, and he decided to get his hands on it. He sent messengers to Padarn with several sacks containing pebbles and moss. The bearers took the sacks to Padarn and told him that they contained the king's treasures. As Maelgwyn was about to engage in a war, the messengers said, he wished Padarn to keep the sacks of treasure safe until he returned home again.

Some months later, Maelgwyn sent his messengers to obtain the treasure sacks. On returning they opened them in the presence of Maelgwyn in order to confirm that the contents were exactly the same as when they were left in their safe keeping. When it was seen that the sacks contained only stones and moss, Maelgwyn's men showed great anger and accused Padarn of being a thief, demanding that the king's sacks should be filled with treasure again.

The Bishop refused and, subsequently, the dispute had to be settled by a trial of ordeal. Padarn and his accusers were ordered to plunge their arms into a cauldron of boiling water. Their arms were then given a short time to heal and then examined. Padarn's arms were found to have healed completely, while those of Maelgwyn's men were still in a raw and painful state, and showed no sign of healing. This was taken as proof that Padarn was innocent and Maelgwyn had to confess his dishonest scheme. He was immediately struck with blindness and a painful disease. However, Padarn healed him on the condition that Maelgwyn would make a grant of all the land between the Clorach and the Rheidol, as a token of true penance, to the church at Llanbadarn.

Llan y Mawddwy, 4 miles north-east of Dinas Mawddwy, Gwynedd
SH 903189 (125)

This little church, peacefully situated in the upper reaches of the Dyfi valley, was founded by St Tydecho, who had the occasional quarrel with Maelgwyn Gwynedd.

One day Maelgwyn sent Tydecho some white horses and requested him to provide some pasture for them. Tydecho, however, did not follow his instructions and turned the horses on to the mountains where they ate the heather and ran wild. When Maelgwyn later sent for his horses, he was horrified to find that they had turned yellow. In a fit of rage, he seized the holy man's oxen in revenge. But Tydecho was not concerned, for he managed to persuade some stags to come out of the forest and allow themselves to be yoked to his plough.

Later that year Maelgwyn Gwynedd came to hunt in the area. One day, feeling tired, he sat on a rock and suddenly found himself stuck to it. He was unable to move until Tydecho had exercised his special powers and released him, but the impression of his behind was left on the rock.

Another rock in the vicinity bears four holes in the shape of a cross which is said to mark the spot where St Tydecho used to kneel in prayer. In his later years he went to live on the Ile de Groix in Brittany where he died and was buried.

Maelgwyn Gwynedd played a prominent part in several of the lives of the saints, for example, St Brynach in Dyfed, St Cattwg in Gwynllwg, St Cybi in Anglesey, St Padarn in Ceredigion and St Tydecho in Powys. They all had encounters with him, which were generally of an unpleasant nature, but despite these problems they all managed to obtain privileges from him for their monastic establishments.

The celebrated bard Taliesin, a regular attender at the King's court, who lived near Geirionydd Lake (Gwynedd), prophesied the death of Maelgwyn Gwynedd in the following lines:

'A strange creature will come
From the marsh of Rhionedd
To punish the crimes
Of Maelgwyn Gwynedd.
Its hair, its teeth
And its eyes all yellow.
'Tis it that shall make
An end of Maelgwyn Gwynedd.'

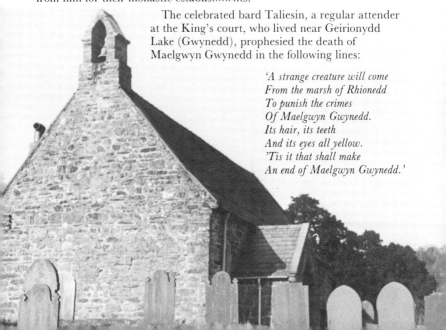

The strange creature with yellow eyes turned out to be the yellow plague which swept through Europe and Britain in the middle of the sixth century.

'It was called the yellow pestilence because those who were attacked by it became yellow; and it appeared to man as a column of watery cloud, having one end trailing along the ground, and the other proceeding in the air and passing through the whole country like a shower going along the bottoms of valleys. Whatever living creature it touched with its pestiferous blast, either died immediately or sickened to death. It attacked the physicians who attended the sick persons. Maelgwyn King of North Wales fell. It attacked beasts also reptiles, and so great was the havoc that the country was almost deserted.'

Liber Landavensis
(The Book of Llandaff)

The yellow fever was certainly a very infectious disease which affected the bilious glands and gave its victim jaundice. It spread to Ireland where two-thirds of the population died from it. Nearly one hundred years later, in 664, it broke out again.

Llanrhôs Church, B5115, near Llandudno, Gwynedd SH 793804 (115)

In an attempt to escape the yellow fever, Maelgwyn hastily laid aside his robes of state and fled over the hills to the church of Eglwys Rhôs where he prostrated himself before the altar, praying earnestly for his life. But it was all in vain, for, like his subjects, he fell victim to the plague and is supposed to have died in the court of Rhôs in 547 A.D. Hence the old adage: 'Hun Maelgwyn yn Eglwys y Rhôs' – 'the sleep of Maelgwyn in Llanrhôs'.

The Maglocunus Stone, Nevern, Dyfed SN 083401 (145)

A stone slab forming a window sill in this church bears an inscription
which reads in Latin and Ogham as follows:

Latin: MAGLOCVNI FILI CLVTOR
Ogham: MAGLICUNAS MAQUI CUTAR

Both these inscriptions translate as:
(The stone of) Maglocunus (Maelgwyn) son of Clutorius.

It is conceivable that this is in fact a memorial stone to Maelgwyn
Gwynedd, although he is generally regarded as the son of Cadwallon
Lawhir and not Clutorius. It is interesting, however, that Gildas in his
sixth-century manuscript referred to Maelgwyn Gwynedd as Maglocunus.

Some say that he is buried in a secret cave in (Gwynedd) Bryn
Maelgwyn, or is interred in Ynys Seiriol (also called Puffin Island), where
the tower of an ancient ruined church stands silhouetted against the sky.

Some excavations were undertaken near the ruined church by Harold
Hughes in 1897 and he later wrote the following description of his finds:

*'On removing the debris of centuries with the aid of a pick and shovel we have
succeeded in making a considerable clearing to the east of the structure. We discovered,
at about four feet from the surface, an ancient tomb. Beneath the rough clay, worn
slabs, and covered with shingle from the shore, lay within a narrow inclosure, with feet
to the east, the skeleton of a man. Although portions of the skeleton had crumbled
away, many fragments remained, and these after much difficulty I pieced together.'*

Was this in fact the tomb of Maelgwyn Gwynedd? The question remains
unanswered.

> *'Who will reign after Maelgwyn?*
> *Rhun is his name, dext'rous his sword-stroke,*
> *Foremost of the army in battle;*
> *Woe is the Britain of the day.'*

Taliesin

Rhun, the eldest son of Maelgwyn Gwynedd, is reputed to have been
illegitimate, but he still managed to succeed his father as ruler of Gwynedd.
His sister Eurgain married Elidyr the Courteous, the son of Gwrwst
Briardar ap Dyfynwal Hen who, on the death of Maelgwyn Gwynedd in

547 A.D., came to North Wales to claim Gwynedd as the inheritance of his wife. A battle was fought near the Cadnant brook to the north-east of Caernarfon, but Elidyr was killed.

In the Triads Rhun is named as one of the three 'Gwyndeyrn' or blessed princes of the Isle of Britain – the other two being Rhuvawn Bevyr and Owain ap Urien. Another Triad links Rhun with Rhiwallon Wallt Banhodden and Cadwaladr Fendigaid, to form the three 'Aurhualogion' or golden-headed ones. It is of significance that the wearing of gold bands around knees, arms and necks were insignia of supreme power in the provinces of Britain. Rhun's chief residence was the Roman fort of Conovium on the western bank of the River Conwy, which, later, took from him its name of Caer Rhun. He died in 586 A.D. and was succeeded by his son Beli.

Dyfed

One of the best known of the early rulers of Dyfed, which retained the old name of Demetia, was Vortepor, the son of Aricol Lawhir. He lived in the sixth century and was a descendant of Magnus Maximus, and was one of the five kings criticized so sourly by Gildas in his epistle *De Excidio Britanniae*, where he was described as the 'tyrant of Demetia'. Gildas spent many years writing this work and it was presented to the world when he was forty-three. It is of particular interest, for it is the only literary work of the sixth century that has survived.

The Voteporix Stone, Carmarthen Museum, Abergwili, Dyfed.

Discovered in the churchyard at Castell Dwyran, this 7 foot stone bears Ogham and Latin inscriptions, which, although they differ slightly, confirm the identity of the honoured person.

VOTECORIGAS (The stone) of Votecorix (Ogham inscription)
MEMORIA / VOTEPORIGIS / PROTICTORIS (Latin inscription)
The memorial of Voteporix the Protector.

Above the Latin inscription is an incised linear ring cross.

Voteporix was probably the king of that name mentioned in the writings of Gildas in the sixth century. He was of Irish descent and became King of Dyfed in 550 A.D. The title of Protector was probably an hereditary title acquired by his family in the Roman period.

'That there should be preserved the monument of a king of South Wales of the first half of the 6th century in such a manner is remarkable. No memorial of any English king of his time survives.'

Sir Cyril Fox

This dynasty ruled over Dyfed until the tenth century. A neighbouring kingdom was Deheubarth, where the last king was Maredudd ap Ewin. He died in 1035 and is commemorated on the Carew Cross (see page 83).

Powys

The ancient kingdom of Powys extended from Mold (now in Clwyd) to Hay-on-Wye. Some writers have claimed that the Powys dynasty was founded by Cadell Ddyrnllug and that the family who ruled this kingdom in the seventh to ninth centuries were his descendants. In the eighth century the ruler was Elise (Eliseg), who is commemorated on the Eliseg pillar cross which stands near the ruins of Valle Crucis Abbey in the Vale of Llangollen (Clwyd).

This long Latin inscription has weathered so badly that it is now impossible to read. Fortunately, it was written down in 1696 by the antiquary Edward Llwyd. It is in 31 horizontal lines (only 7 can be seen now) and the translation is as follows:

†Concenn son of Catell, Catell
son of Brochmail, Brochmail son
of Eliseg, Eliseg son of Guoillauc
†Concenn therefore being great-grandson of Eliseg
erected this stone to his great-grandfather
Eliseg † It is Eliseg who annexed
the inheritance of Powys . . .
throughout nine (years) from the power of the English
which he made into a sword-land by fire
† Whosoever shall read this hand-inscribed inscription
stone, let him give a blessing on
the soul of Eliseg † It is Concenn
Who . . . with his hand

. . . to his own kingdom of Powys

. . . and which

. . .

. . . the mountain

. . .

. . . the monarchy

Maximus . . . of Britain . . .

Concenn, Pascent, . . . Maun, Annan.

† Britu, moreover, (was) the son of Guorthigirn (Vortigern)

Whom Germanus blessed and

whom Severa bore to him, the daughter of Maximus

the king who slew the king of the Romans and

† Conmarch painted this writing at the command of his king

Concenn

† The blessing of the Lord (be) upon Concenn and all members of

his family

and upon all the land of Powys

Until the day of judgement. Amen.

Eliseg was the tenth generation of this Powys dynasty and he lived in the middle of the eighth century. His grandson Cattell died in 808 A.D. and was succeeded by Concenn or Cyngen who erected this pillar cross in memory of his great-grandfather. This suggests that the cross was erected in the first half of the ninth century, for Concenn died in about 854 A.D. during a pilgrimage to Rome.

King Vortigern and his son Britu are given special mention, and also Pascent, who was Vortigern's third son. It is of interest that Nennius, writing in 822 A.D., records that the later kings of Buellt (now Builth Wells) and Gwerthrynion – sub kingdoms of Powys – were descended from Pascent. What may have been his memorial stone was found at Tywyn in the eighteenth century. It was inscribed with the name Pascentius, but this was quite a common Christian-Roman name and may not necessarily signify the same one. The stone was subsequently lost.

The ancestors of Concenn and Eliseg are no doubt mentioned on the pillar to demonstrate their importance. In particular they claimed descent from the Roman Emperor Magnus Maximus, who was formerly a Roman official of Spanish origin stationed in Britain as governor. He became the 'Maxen Wledig' in the traditional stories of Wales.

Concenn was the last king of the line and, when he died, Rhodri Mawr ('the Great') inherited Powys through his mother Nest, the sister of Concenn, who married Merfyn Frych (Concenn's father).

Rhodri Mawr (the Great) was the central figure of the ninth century. He united the Welsh princes against the Norsemen and defeated the sea rovers in a great battle, killing Horm their leader. Alfred of Wessex, who was living at this time, was also extolled as 'Great' by his people.

Rhodri then married the sister of the King of Cardigan and became ruler of all south-west Wales with the exception of Dyfed. By making politically desirable marriages it was possible for the rulers of these times to acquire neighbouring kingdoms and increase the size of their domains without drawing the sword.

He died in 878 A.D., by which time he was the ruler of the greater part of Wales, with the exception of Brycheiniog, Dyfed, Gwent and Glamorgan. His extensive kingdom was divided among three of his sons who gave a great deal of harassment to the South Wales dynasty. Rhodri's son Cadell became the ruler of Ceredigion, but he died in 909 A.D. and his territory was inherited by Hywel, who later became known as Hywel Dda ('the Good'). On the death of Idwal Foel, a grandson of Rhodri Mawr, Gwynedd and Powys also became the domain of Hywel, and in due course he married Elen, the daughter of Llywarch of Dyfed, in order to extend his kingdom even further. From 942 A.D. he ruled over the whole of Wales with the exception of Glamorgan and Gwent.

Hywel Dda was famous for the introduction of a set of laws which were enforced throughout Wales, and when he died in 950 A.D., after a reign of comparative peace, Wales once more became a divided land with several rulers.

It is possible that Hywel Dda's memorial stone is the inscribed pillar stone bearing a Latin ring cross that can be seen at St Gwnws's church at Llanwnws in Dyfed (see page 112).

The long inscription on the pillar of Eliseg is unique in Britain as an Early Christian epitaph, and it is most unfortunate that its importance was not recognized at an early date and the monument given protection from the elements. Fortunately, Edward Llwyd had the foresight to make a record of its message to the world.

Castell Dinas Bran, Llangollen, Clwyd SJ 223430 (117)

'The castle of the fort of Bran' occupies a dramatic position on the summit of a conical hill dominating the Vale of Llangollen. Bran, who lived a few hundred years before King Arthur, is said to have once occupied an early fortification on this site. In later years Dinas Bran became a stronghold of Eliseg, a prince of Powys who ruled in the 8th century.

'The castelle of Dinas Brane was never a bygge thing, but sette al for strength in a place half inaccessible for ennemyes.'

Leland, Itinerary

The castle of Bran was an important site, being the key to the valley of the Dee and one of the principal gateways into the heart of Wales. During the Middle Ages it was held by the prince of Powys – the middle kingdom which lay between Gwynedd in the north and Dehubarth in the south. When the principality of Powys ceased to exist, Dinas Bran castle passed into the hands of the Trevor family who were lords of Chirk for a long period.

The Pillar of Eliseg, Powys

Meifod Church (A495), 4 miles south of Llanfyllin, Powys SJ 154132 (125)

Inside this church is a roughly carved Celtic pillar with figures depicted on it. At present the stone stands at the west end of the south aisle, but it previously stood at the north end of the central aisle, where it is believed to have covered a vault; it was removed from that position in 1838. It is quite possible that the stone is a memorial to a prince of Powys.

The original church was built by St Gwyddfarch at the west end of the churchyard. Then in 600–650 A.D. St Tysilio, the son of Brochwel Ysgythrog, Prince of Powys, built a new church at Meifod – probably between the present one and St Gwyddfarch's construction.

In the period 750–800 A.D., after the loss of Shrewsbury and the building of Offa's Dyke, Mathrafal became a residence of the princes of Powys and Meifod was the chief religious centre of the area. The present church was erected in the twelfth century and developed in 1500.

It is quite possible that the Meifod Stone commemorates Madog, the eldest son of Meredydd ab Bleddyn, Prince of Powys. His name was given to Powys Fadog, one of the divisions of Powys.

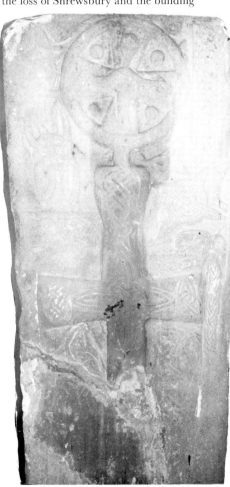

Brychan of Brycheiniog

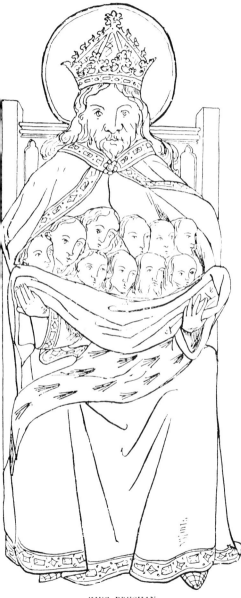

KING BRYCHAN
From stained glass, S. Neot's, Cornwall

Brychan, whose name is now associated with Brecon in Powys, was the son of Prince Anlach, the son of King Coromac of Ireland. His mother was Queen Marchel, the daughter of King Tewdrig. The name Brychan is derived from Brych, which means spotted, so he was perhaps a man with many freckles. He certainly had many children, for he is accredited with twenty-four sons and twenty-four daughters, all produced from three marriages, to Prawst, Rigrawst and Roistri. According to the Welsh Triads, Brychan 'brought up his children and grandchildren in learning and the liberal arts, that they might be able to show the faith in Christ to the nation of the Cymry'. The family of Brychan Brycheiniog were so revered for their saintliness that they were mentioned in the Triads as one of the three holy families of Britain. Most of the offspring made their mark in the world and are listed among the Welsh saints and martyrs.

The Artbeu Stone, St Tydfil's Church, Merthyr Tydfil, Mid Glamorgan SN 049058 (160)

The martyred sons included Arthen, who was murdered and buried at Merthyr Tydfil, where an inscribed stone bearing the name Artbeu can be seen; and Cynan, who was murdered by the Saxons, and is buried at Cynon Merthyr (Powys). Two other well-known sons were Rhun, who inherited his father's domain and is buried at Llandevaelog, and Dingad, who founded churches at Llandingat and Llandovery (Dyfed).

Some of his notable daughters were: Gwladus, who married Gwynlliw and was the mother of Cattwg; Tydfil, who was murdered at Merthyr Tydfil; Meleri, who became the wife of Ceredig and the mother of Sandde, the father of St David; Llud, who was martyred at Slwch Tump near Brecon by a Saxon chieftain and later buried at Usk; and Gwen, who was murdered by Saxons and buried in Talgarth.

The main court of Brychan's territory was at Garth Madrun, which today is known as Talgarth. There was another stronghold at Trecastell and also one at Ystrad Yw in the Rhiangoll Valley of the Black Mountains. This name was later given to a district that formed the south-eastern corner of Brycheiniog.

On Brychan's death his territory was divided between two of his sons – Cledwyn and Rhun. This divided kingdom was later unified under Brychan's grandson, Caradoc Freichfras (Caradoc of the Brawny Arm), who lived in the early sixth century and was said to have been one of the knights of King Arthur. His exploits in the battle of Cattraeth are preserved in the poem called 'The Gododin'. Caradoc was succeeded by his son Cawrdaf who, in the Triads, is named as one of the Three Prime Ministers of Britain. The grave of Brychan is said to be on the island of Ynys Brychan, near Man.

The Grave of Anlach (Brychan's Father), Llanspydid Church, near Brecon, Powys SN 012282 (160)

An ancient stone with a ring cross carved on it is reputed to mark the grave of Anlach, who was the son of King Coramac of Ireland. He married Marchell, the daughter of King Tewdric (see page 137).

The stone bears a small Maltese cross in a circle, with smaller circles on the outside and one in the centre. It was accidentally broken about a hundred years ago when a fire was lit nearby. The fragments were later pieced together.

N.B. The church of Llanhamlach to the east of Brecon is probably derived from the name of Anlach.

Gwynlliw of Gwynlliwg

St Woolos Cathedral, Newport, Gwent ST 309876 (171)

On Allt Wynllyw, now known as Stow Hill, stands the church of Eglwys Wynllw. This site was once the fortified home of Gwynlliw, one of the sons of Glwys who ruled over an extensive kingdom west of the Usk. When Glwys died his territory was split into two districts which were given to his sons to administer. Gwynlliw became ruler of this area between the Rhymni and Usk rivers which became known as Gwynlliw-wg, later shortened to Gwynlliwg and eventually corrupted to Wentlooge.

Gwynlliw sent his respectful compliments to Brychan of Brycheiniog and requested permission to marry his daughter Gwladys. But Brychan refused, so Gwynlliw decided to use force. Accompanied by three hundred men, he crossed the Black Mountains and descended on Brychan's court at Talgarth and captured young Gwladys.

On discovering that his daughter was missing, Brychan set off in pursuit and caught up with them at Bochriwcarn (Fochriw) where, by chance, they met up with King Arthur and two of his knights, Kai and Bedwr. Arthur was so struck by the beauty of Gwladys that he was strongly inclined to capture her himself, but he was dissuaded from doing so by his two noble knights. They then gave assistance to Gwynlliw and persuaded Brychan to return to Garth Madrun (Talgarth).

Gwynlliw and Gwladys then completed their journey to the fort on Allt Gwynlliw where in due course Gwladys gave birth to a son named Cattwg (Cadoc), who was to become one of the best known saints in Wales. As a young man he studied at Caerwent under Tatheus (St Tathan). He subsequently converted his parents to Christianity, persuading Gwynlliw to establish a simple church near his fort on Allt Wynnliw.

The site of the original church is marked by the ancient chapel of St Mary which is between the tower and the later church. This chapel is about 15 yards long and it is probable that as founder, Gwynlliw is buried beneath the floor.

Gwladys left her husband to live near the river Ebbw a few miles away where she set up an oratory. Later she moved on to Pencarnau (a hill fort near Bassaleg) and in later years founded a church (Capel Wladus) near Gelligaer (see page 165).

No memorial stone has ever been discovered that bears any reference to Gwynlliw, but a stone slab bearing a Celtic cross found at Capel Gwladys in Mid Glamorgan (see page 165) may be a memorial stone to his wife Gwladys. Their son Cattwg may possibly have been commemorated on a stone found at Llandefaelog fach church in Powys (see page 101).

Examples of forgotten courts and fortresses of the Dark Ages

Aberffraw SH 354688 (114)
Here the kings of Gwynedd had their main court for nearly 600 years, but no trace of it can be seen today. It was certainly used as a royal residence by Rhoderic the Great in 870 A.D., and Llewelyn the Last, Prince of North Wales, had a palace here at the time of his death in 1282 A.D.

Bodysgollen, near Llanrhos SH 798794 (115)
This old house takes its name from the abode (bod) of Caswallon Lawhir, the father of Maelgwyn Gwynedd, who had a palace here a short distance from the present building.

Mathrafl, Powys SJ 132107
Just above the junction of the Banw and Vyrnwy, but on the Banw, are the mounds that mark the site of a former headquarters of the kings of Powys. They form a quadrangle with a tump at one corner immediately above the river Banw.

Plas Cadnant in Gwynedd
This is said to have once been the site of the home of the mother of Rhodri the Great.

Llyswarney, Vale of Glamorgan SS 963742 (170)
It is said that an ancient town once stood here and within it was the palace of Nudd Hael, who lived here in the sixth century and was apparently a very rich man.

Y Gaer yn Arfon (Caernarfon) SH 486623 (115)
This ancient Welsh fortification became the Segontium of the Romans and is known as Caernarfon. Constantine the Great is buried here, and it was also the home of Elen of the Hosts, the British wife of the Emperor Maximus. The fort on the hill of Llanbeblig was the ancient centre of the Cantref and the original home of its chieftains.

Dinefawr near Llandeilo Fawr
This ancient fortress on a hill overlooking the Twi was once the royal residence of the princes of Dheubarth.

8.
On the Trail
of King Arthur

Just who was Uther or Uther Pendragon? This is the key question in any search for the ubiquitous King Arthur, for by clearly identifying the father it should be possible to then easily trace the son. If there was an Uther Pendragon, and Arthur was his son, then the pair of them should be easily traceable.

A. T. Blackett and A. Wilson, 1984

In every part of Britain one encounters stories of King Arthur and his amazing deeds. An enormous number of books have been written about this subject, although even the question of his existence has been doubted. However, most historians now agree that he did exist, but apart from the well-known spoof discovery by the Glastonbury monks in 1190, no one, until recently, has made a serious attempt to identify King Arthur's burial site or to explain very convincingly how he fits into history.

In 1983 reports of a remarkable claim that the grave of Arthur had been discovered in south-east Wales were published in *The Western Mail, The Guardian* and *The Daily Mail* among other newspapers. Two amateur historians, Alan Wilson and A. T. (Mick) Blackett, had been working together for about eight years on this project. Their work is the result of a mammoth research programme which might be described as a piece of historical detective work.

By linking together overlapping pieces of evidence obtained from books and manuscripts that exist in many varied and scattered sources, they have reconstructed a 'family tree' of Dark Age dynasties in Wales, covering the period from 50 B.C. to 1100 A.D.. In their research they came to the conclusion that when Geoffrey of Monmouth was compiling his *History of Britain* in the twelfth century, from a jumbled and ancient mass of information, he managed to confuse two great kings, compounding them into one mighty and mysterious monarch. Geoffrey failed to realize that there were, in fact, two important kings who bore the name of Arthur. The first one died in 388 A.D. and the second Arthur lived from around 500 to 575 A.D. This was how the confusion surrounding the identity of Arthur first began, and up to now few people have realized it.

The legends of King Arthur have become firmly established in Cornwall during the last few hundred years and it is significant that this may be entirely due to the misidentification of an area named Cerniw. Blackett and Wilson claim that this has produced:

the biggest red herring in all history, and combined with the guesswork of John Leland, the king's antiquarian of 1530 A.D., it has resulted in a transfer to a foreign land. Leland literally guessed that Cadbury Hill was Camelot and also that the battle of Camlan was fought in Cornwall, and so he compounded the forgery of the Glastonbury monks that Arthur was buried at that Abbey.

Cerniw appears many times in the old manuscripts and like all ancient names it has many spellings. It is alternatively Cerniw, Cernyw, Kerniw, Kernyw, Gernyw and so on, but in the end it is Cerniw. It is a very special word, for it is in Cerniw that the great war king of the British nation had his main military camp. This was the camp fort at Gelly Wig, and here King Arthur gathered his armies. The mediaeval writers in England translated the name Cerniw as Cornwall – for it looked something similar. Well, Cerniw is where it has always been – in South East Wales; it is still marked on the Ordnance Survey maps, lying along the border area of Gwent and Glamorgan.

St Ceinwr was a great-grandson of King Caradoc and he founded Llangeinwr in Gwent, and this area took its name Cerniw from Ceinwr. Later, Cerniw was ruled by a minor King, Glywys ap Tegid, around 450 A.D., and it became Glywysswg. When his son King Gwynlliw ap Glywys [see page 132] ruled, it became Gwynlliwg, which was subsequently corrupted to Wentlooge. When Cerniw in South Wales was confused with Cornwall, this played a major part in obscuring the epic story of King Arthur and his people.

A. T. Blackett and A. Wilson, 1984

Tintern Abbey, A466, Gwent SO 533000 (162)

In the *Book of Llandaff* the story is related of how the elderly King Tewdrig went into retirement at Din Teyryn, where he held a small fortification near the site of Tintern Abbey (Tintern being a corruption of Din Teyryn). The Saxons invaded and Tewdrig took up arms to come to the aid of his son Meurig, and a great battle was fought at Pont y Saeson (the Bridge of the Saxons) nearby. They won the battle, but old Tewdrig was mortally wounded. He was taken on a cart drawn by two oxen to have his wounds tended, but he died at a place which is now known as Mathern and here he was buried. Subsequently, a church was constructed over his grave, which lies beneath the north wall of the chancel. This was excavated in 1610 A.D. by Bishop Godwin who discovered a stone coffin containing Tewdrig's bones.

Mathern Church, near Chepstow, Gwent ST 523910 (162)

The name of this church is derived from Merthyr Teyryn, which means 'the Martyr King'. It is the burial site of King Tewdrig who Blackett and Wilson claim was King Arthur's grandfather. He bore the title 'Uther Pendragon', which means 'Wonderful Commander'; this title was also given to his son Meurig and Arthur himself.

'A church is said to have been erected on its present site (Mathern) by Meurig or Maurice who is supposed to be the father of the Arthur so renowned in British story.'

Archdeacon W. Coxe, 1801

Tewdrig's son Meurig was the father of King Arthur, and Blackett and Wilson claim that he is buried in Llandaff Cathedral, near Cardiff. They say that he lies in a tomb close to the altar on the right-hand side of God. Rebuilt several times, this cathedral has a long history. St Teilo lies on the south side opposite St Dyfrig (Dubricious), whose remains were brought here from Bardsey Island in 1120 and reburied here at Llandaff by Bishop Urban. Dyfrig is supposed to have crowned Arthur at Caerleon in 518 A.D.

So Arthwyr (Arthur) is shown to be the 37th king of Glamorgan and Gwent, who subsequently became King of all Britain. He was the son of King Meurig and Queen Onbrawst, brother of Idnerth and Frioc. His uncle was St Dyfrig (Dubricious), and two of his cousins were St Illtud and St Cattwg, who are both very familiar names in South Wales. Arthwyr was the father of Ithael, Gwaednerth, Nowi and Morgan. The latter son subsequently ruled the kingdom of Morgannwg which was the land of Gwent and Glamorgan as it is today.

'Morcant or Morgan succeeded his father Arthwyr, Arthur or Uther and was the 38th King of Gwent . . . he is celebrated as a model of piety and virtue and his manners have affixed to him the appellation of Morgan Mwynvawr or Morgan the Courteous.'

David Williams' History of Monmouthshire, 1784.

The immediate descent of Arthwyr is shown as follows:

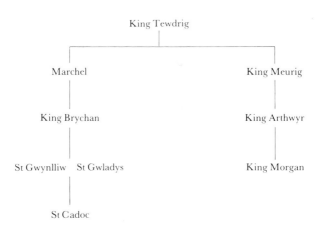

King Tewdrig

Marchel — King Meurig

King Brychan — King Arthwyr

St Gwynlliw   St Gwladys — King Morgan

St Cadoc

'Arthur was the son of Meurig ap Tewdrig, a prince of the Silurian Britons at the commencement of the sixth century, and who is, in all probability, to be identified with our hero's reputed sire, Uthyr or Uther of legendary celebrity.'

The Cambrian Plutarch, John J. Parry, 1834

Blackett and Wilson claim that Arthur's name in its various forms (Arthmael, Antorious, for example) appears on several inscribed stones that can be seen in Glamorgan, and that several of these stones also show his name in conjunction with the names of his nieces, nephews, cousins and other contemporaries.

One such example is the Pumpeius stone, which can be seen in Margam museum. Originally, it stood two miles south of Kenfig, just north of the ruins of the castle. It is inscribed: PVMEIUS CAR ANTORIVS which they believe translates – 'Pompey the kinsman of Arthur'. Pompey (or Poppai or Poppey) was the fourth son of King Brychan of Brycheiniog. Alternatively, it may refer to a contemporary of Arthur – King Howell or Riwal, who ruled Dumnonia in Brittany and called himself Pompeius Regalis. He was a king who is supposed to have brought his army over to Britain to fight at Arthur's side.

Lodge Hill, Caerleon, Gwent ST 322914 (171)

Situated 400 feet above the River Usk are the fortifications of an Iron Age fortress which Blackett and Wilson suggest was re-occupied in the sixth century by King Arthur. Lodge may be derived from Llys, meaning court. This site has never been excavated and it would be fascinating if evidence of Dark Age occupation came to light, such as has been shown at Dinas Powis, near Cardiff, and at Deganwy, near Conwy.

The fort is situated at the highest point of a ridge which stretches between Malpas and Caerleon and overlooks the River Usk. On the southern side is an old Roman road leading from Caerleon to Newport. The main enclosure is protected by three massive ramparts which in some places are 30 feet deep. The whole camp measures 440 yards long and is about 175 yards wide.

Camlan, A458, east of Dolgellau, Gwynedd SH 815163 (124)

There has always been a great deal of argument and conjecture over the possible site of Arthur's last battle at Camlan, where he was supposed to have been mortally wounded. One version of the story claims that the stricken king was borne to Tintagel after the battle, and all the time that he lay dying the sea and winds moaned unceasingly until he was buried at Glastonbury. Other suggestions have been made that the battle site was at the Roman fort of Camaglanna, by Hadrian's Wall in Northumberland, or near the River Cam in Somerset.

Blackett and Wilson firmly believe that Camlan is a place of that very name, now on the A458, in the pass of Ochr-yr-Bwlch to the east of Dolgellau. It is still so named on the present edition of the Ordnance Survey map. It was once an important pass link between North and South Wales in the Afon Cerist valley; it is crooked in shape and indeed the name means 'crooked glen'. They also have good reasons for believing that Arthur fought a battle in this location.

According to popular legend, Arthur is not dead but is merely sleeping in a cave and will one day return. The cave in question has been variously located in Northumberland, Cumberland, Yorkshire, Cheshire, Somerset, and in at least four different parts of Wales. The mystery surrounding Arthur's last resting place certainly explains the traditional stories that 'he lived on'; perhaps this was the intention, for when he died he was in fact hidden. A poem in *The Mabinogion* concerning the memorials of the graves of the warriors gives the details of the burial sites of numerous important chieftains, but it firmly states: 'But unknown is the grave of Arthur.'

142

Blackett and Wilson claim to have worked out the final solution to this mystery by following what has been stated in ancient manuscripts and sorting out the clues on the ground. By interpreting a well-known folk tale which concerns the burial of King Arthur in a Welsh cave, they are convinced that they have worked out where this took place. This extract is from the writings of Nennius who compiled a manuscript entitled *History of the Britons* in 822 A.D.:

'St Illtud was praying in a cave, the mouth of which is towards the sea and he beheld a ship sailed towards him from the sea and two men sailing in it. And the body of a holy man was with them in the ship and an altar above his face, which was held up by the will of God. And the man of God went forth to meet them and the body of the holy man, and the altar was inseparably continuing above the face of the holy body. And they said to St Illtud "This man of God entrusted to us, that we should conduct him to thee and that we should bury him with thee and that thou shouldst not reveal his name to any man, so that men should not swear by him."

And they buried him and after the burial these two men returned to the ship and set sail.'

This is an account of a secret burial in Glamorgan at the same time that King Arthur disappears, and where his first cousin St Illtud is the undertaker.

To quote Alan Wilson:

'In a land where all important burials of important people were a matter of common knowledge and recorded in song and poetry, any secret burial is an extraordinary event. It is totally alien to the entire philosophy and culture of the nation. As we know where King Tewdric, the grandfather of Arthur, lies buried, and we can be equally sure of the burial place of King Meurig his father and King Morgan his son, we are left with King Arthur as the only candidate for a midnight burial. In fact, King Arthur is the only king who is recorded as being buried somewhere unknown.'

St Illtud's secret cave, Coed y Mwstwr Wood, Mid Glamorgan.
(Grid reference not for publication)

The secret burial cave is in Coed y Mwstwr wood, where King Arthur was concealed in a rock tomb hewn out of solid rock. It measures about 4 feet across by 10 feet deep. The axis of the grave along its 10 foot length lies east-to-west in accordance with Christian practice.

The final problem was to locate the reburial site, for it could be assumed that the body of Arthur had been removed from the cave at a later date and buried in a more fitting location. By following a further series of clues that included two mediaeval accounts that told of the burial of the 'Uther Pendragon' at Caer Caradoc, and by utilizing a mass of corroborative evidence, they were able to identify this particular location in the centre of Glamorgan, where a ruined church stands on a hilltop. Here they searched for further clues and made the following discovery:

'One day we were about to pack up and go home when we uncovered a strange looking stone, partially buried, and covered in moss and with a shoulder shape at one end. Blackett was convinced that the shoulder angle looked unnatural – in fact manmade – and so in the gloom and dusk we heaved and tugged to get at the stone. Scratching away at it, we convinced ourselves that there were some markings on it. But the light had gone so we covered it up and decided to return in daylight and have another look.

'The next day we returned and removed the rest of the moss and mud to reveal an inscription, and we immediately realized that we had found the stone of King Arthur, son of Meurig, and the search was over.'

The inscribed memorial stone carries the inscription REX ARTORIUS FILI MAURICIUS which means BRENHIN ARTHWYR AP MEURIG in Welsh and translates as 'King Arthur son of Maurice (Meurig)' in English.

The style of the lettering ties in with other sixth-century stones, and it is most intriguing that the stone is sword-shaped.

Three substantial volumes have been published by Blackett and Wilson, putting forward their exciting theories and claims. The whole project has involved them in a personal cost of nearly £60,000 which they have raised by selling their houses and other possessions, a measure of their commitment and belief in the validity of their discoveries. Their books, which have been published as limited first editions, are:
King Arthur of Gwent and Glamorgan, King Arthur and the Charters of the King and *Arthur the War King*. A fourth volume entitled *King Arthur's Invisible Kingdom* will be published in due course.

'If the findings are correct history books will have to be re-written and South Wales will have several extra tourist attractions.'

Paul Hoyland
The Guardian, 23 July 1983

9.
Celtic Saints
and Holy Places

'St Govan, he built him a cell
By the side of the Pembroke sea
And there, as the crannied sea-gulls dwell
In a tiny secret citadel
He sighed for eternity . . .'

St Govan
A. G. Prys-Jones, 1888

St Govan's Chapel, south of Pembroke at St Govan's Head, Dyfed. SS
967929 (158)

During the fifth and sixth centuries the whole of Wales was Christianized by the wandering holy men and women of the Celtic Church, later dubbed 'Saints', although not officially canonized by the Church of Rome.

The total number of known Welsh saints is about five hundred, but there are also 20,000 said to be buried on the Isle of Enlli (Bardsey)! Ireland and Wales had as many saints as all the rest of Christendom put together.

The Celtic saint was rather different from his equivalent in the Latin Church. He, or she, was a person who had entered the ecclesiastical profession and was regarded as a saint irrespective of moral qualities – saints by vocation, but not always by their way of life. Piro, the Abbot of Caldey, for example, was a drunk who one day ended his career by tumbling into a well and drowning, although he was still later regarded as a saint. This period of Welsh history is known as 'the age of the saints'; it was a time of intellectual and spiritual development when close links were formed with Brittany (Amorica).

Circular Churchyards

From the days of the arrival of the first Celtic people in Britain the dead were buried within the sign of the circle, as is evidenced by the round barrows, stone circles and enclosures of many ancient churches. Graves were marked by the symbol of the circle in pre-Christian times in the same way that the cross was used as a burial symbol in later times.

The word llan signifies an enclosure or fenced-in area, and was originally a reference to the churchyard rather than the sacred building. It is quite possible that the word reflects memories of worship once held within stone circles.

Examples of circular churchyards in Wales may be seen at the following churches:
Llanelidan, Efenechtyd, Llandyrnog, Tremeirchion, Cilcaen, Llan-armon, Cerrig-y-drudion, Bettws Gwerfil Goch (Clwyd); Llangely-nin, Llaneltud (Gwynedd); Pennant Melangell, Llanilltud (Powys); and Kilgwrrwg (Gwent).It is on record that Patrick, Bishop of the Hebrides (Scotland), desired Orlygus to build a church wherever

he found the upright stones or menhirs. It may be demonstrated that in Wales many churches were also built near megaliths.

Yspytty Cynfyn near Devil's Bridge in Dyfed SN753791 (135) is a classic example of a church built within a stone circle. In the photograph the stones can be seen at regular intervals incorporated into the churchyard wall. There are also stone pillars at the eastern entrance to the churchyard.

In ancient times any fugitive who came into a church enclosure could claim the right of sanctuary for seven years and seven days. This was the circle of God's protection – not of the dead, but of the living, no matter how guilty they were.

Kilgwrrwg Church, near Devauden, Gwent ST 463984 (171)

A little church situated in a circular Celtic churchyard in the middle of a field. It is remotely placed but is still used regularly for worship.

St Curig's Staff, St Harmon's Church, between Llanidloes and Rhyader, Powys SO 989728 (147)

Inside this church there used to be preserved a pastoral staff that was supposed to have belonged to St Curig, the founder of Llangurig church. Giraldus Cambrensis, in his *Itinerary Through Wales*, written in 1188, described this staff as follows:

'In the church of St Germanus there is a staff of Saint Cyric, covered on all sides with gold and silver, and resembling in its upper part the form of a cross; its efficacy has been proved in many cases, but particularly in the removal of glandular and strumous swellings; insomuch that all persons afflicted with these complaints, on a devout application to the staff, with the oblation of one penny, are restored to health. But it happened in these our days, that a strumous patient on presenting one halfpenny to the staff, the humour subsided only in the middle; but when the oblation was completed by the other halfpenny, an entire cure was accomplished. Another person also coming to the staff with the promise of a penny, was cured; but not fulfilling his engagement on the day appointed, he relapsed into his former disorder; in order, however, to obtain pardon for his offence, he tripled the offering by presenting three-pence, and thus obtained a complete cure.'

It appears that the miraculous staff was destroyed during the Reformation.

St Harmon's church was founded by Garmon or Germanus early in the fifth century. It is reputed that the saint and his followers prayed here against the wicked sins of Vortigern (see page 114). The church, like many in this part of Wales, stands on a prehistoric mound within a circular churchyard, suggesting that it was originally a fortified site.

The Selection of Sacred Sites

There are many legends in different parts of Wales in which spirits or some other mysterious powers play a prominent part in the removal of churches from one site to another, persuading the 'architect' to pick a more suitably sacred location.

Llanddeusant church near Llandovery in Dyfed was originally to have been built at Twynllanan, in the centre of the parish, but the stones that were placed there during the day were apparently removed during the night to the location where the church now stands.

Near Llanbister church in Powys is a piece of land where the construction of the building was first commenced, but during the night the stones kept disappearing, so another site was chosen.

When the first attempts were made to build Llanwinio church in Dyfed, everything that was put up during the day fell down in the night, until at last the builder threw his hammer into the air; the church was then built on the spot where the hammer landed and work progressed without any hindrance.

In the middle of Llangan parish in Dyfed there is a field called Parc-y-Fynwent where, according to local tradition, the church was to have originally been built. But the stones brought to the spot by day were removed by invisible hands in the night to the place where the church now stands. A voice was heard saying 'Llanga dyma'r fon' (Llangan here is the spot).

Similar stories to these few examples are told in many other locations in Wales.

The Thumb Shaped Stone, Corwen Church, Gwynedd SJ 078434 (125)

This stone can be seen in the north porch wall and is known as the 'pointed stone in the cold corner'. According to a local story, when the church was being built, a voice was heard calling out a warning that no building would remain standing until a different site was chosen, and this must be near a large stone. It would seem that this advice was followed and a new site chosen – where the church now stands. The standing stone was incorporated into the wall of the porch at a later date.

Llanwrth Church, near Rhyader, Powys SN 975636 (141)

A large hunk of stone stands near the entrance to the church. It may safely be assumed that the stone was here long before the church was erected. Other examples may be seen at Maentwrog and Corwen in Gwynedd (see page 151).

Llantilio Crossenny Church, east of Abergavenny, Gwent SO
398149 (161)

The parish church of Llantilio Crossenny is built on an artificial mound
within the site of an ancient fort. Many churches in Wales are built on
artificial mounds and frequently within ancient fortifications. Other
examples may be seen at Caergybi Gwynedd (see page 162), Pendine,
Tregaron, Llandewi Brefi (Dyfed).

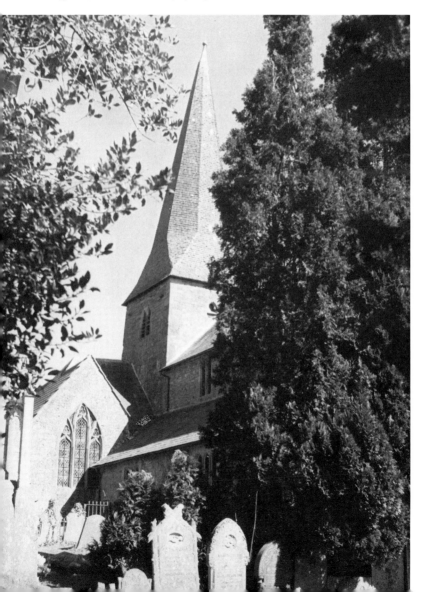

Early Monasteries and Seats of Learning

The first monasteries of Wales were not great stone buildings but a collection of mud and wattle huts where the monks lived near the main church, which was generally built of wood with a roof of rushes. Small handbells were rung to call the monks to worship inside the church where the services were read and sung in Latin, the language used by the church throughout Europe. The monks spent a large proportion of their time in agricultural work, producing food to meet the needs of the community. They also undertook woodwork, metalwork and weaving. Instruction was given in the scriptures, geometry, grammar, classical literature and all aspects of philosophy.

From these monastic institutions the monks would set out on missionary journeys, sometimes accompanied by small bands of followers. They would stop at settlements and preach to the people. If accepted, they would settle there and erect a small hut as a church. This would be enclosed by a ditch and a simple rampart – an area known as a llan (enclosure), a word now used to signify a church.

Bede, writing in the tenth century, provided the following information on the establishment of the early churches:

'They would remain there in constant prayer and fast for forty days and nights. They would eat only a small amount after sunset and on Sundays when a small piece of bread, one egg and a little water would be consumed. At the end of that period the place became the property of the holy man and it was called henceforth after his name.'

These simple churches were usually located in valleys near streams or springs (which were often in later times regarded as holy wells), for a good water supply was an essential consideration.

Many of these primitive churches subsequently fell into ruin and were never replaced, but the majority were, in due course, rebuilt several times to become, finally, the parish churches of today.

These early Christian missionaries were energetic travellers who often made long and dangerous journeys to preach the Gospel, and they made visits to other lands such as Brittany, parts of Germany and even Iceland. They were very brave men and women who endured considerable danger and hardship. The age of the saints will always be remembered for the names of people such as Dewi,

Cybi, Padarn, Fraed, Non, Illtud, Cattwg and a host of others have been perpetuated in hundreds of churches throughout Wales.

The lives of the saints were generally written up at least 600 years after the time of their lifetime; and consequently, the accounts are full of magical and exaggerated stories.

Llan Illtud (Llantwit Major), South Glamorgan SS 966687 (170)

This is one of the most fascinating churches in Wales, for not only does it contain several interesting inscribed and decorated stones, but it is situated near the site of the once renowned college of St Illtud.

The settlement was originally known as Caer Wrgan and later Côr Eurgain (Eurgain's Choir or College) where Eurgain, the daughter of Caradoc (Caractacus), established a small college of twenty-four monks in the third century (or so it is reputed). The college was redeveloped in the fourth century by the Roman General Theodosius (known by the Welsh as Tewdws) and it was renamed Côr Tewdws. Balerius, a Roman Christian, was the principal teacher. For a while the college continued to expand until it was attacked by Irish pirates. It then remained in ruins for about one hundred years until Garmon came from Brittany in about 450 A.D.

155

and refounded the establishment. A young Breton monk named Illtud was appointed principal and under his direction the college flourished. In due course it became the most important Christian educational establishment in Britain, known as Bangor Illtud. The present name of the town is a corruption of Llan Illtud – the church of Illtud.

It has been called the 'Pompeii of the Saints' and it can certainly be claimed that more 'saints' set out from this holy seat of learning between the fifth and tenth centuries than any other religious centre in Wales. St Illtud not only taught wisdom and theology but also the techniques of agriculture, and he even designed a new type of plough. It is claimed that there were once seven kings' sons in residence at the college at the same time. Two thousand students could be accommodated in four hundred timber huts and seven halls. St Illtud's more famous pupils included Samson, Gildas, Aurelian, Dewi and Maelgwyn Gwynedd.

The remains of Bangor Illtud are scattered over a wide area in the vicinity of Llantwit Major church. Several roads lead out from the town which signifies its importance. One of them is the Via Julia, which ran from the old Roman fort of Bovium to Kenfig, Margam and Neath.

Following the era of St Illtud, the college was in operation for a considerable period of time. It went into decline in the eleventh century, however, when Robert Fitzhaman transferred a large proportion of the college revenues to the abbey at Tewkesbury. At the time of the Reformation it still existed, but its prosperity was undermined when the remaining endowments were transferred to Gloucester Cathedral.

Llanveithin, near Llancarfan, south of Bonvilston, off A48, South
Glamorgan SS 052703 (170)

St Cattwg (also known as Cadoc or Cadfael) came to the Carfan valley in
the sixth century and set up a small fortification which became known as
Castell Cattwg. He constructed a simple church nearby with a group of
huts to house his followers. From these humble beginnings Llancarfan
grew into an important seat of learning. Cattwg's reputation as a wise man
spread and many came here to study under him. He was the son of
Gwynlliw, born in about 497 A.D., and heir to the kingdom of Gynllwg, but
he had no desire to take up his inheritance and devoted his life instead to
study and religion. The monastery at Llancarfan became one of the three
great monastic establishments within the Diocese of Llandaff and one of
the largest in Wales. Cattwg was known as Cattwg Doeth ('the Wise')

*'He (Cattwg) fed daily a hundred clergymen, a hundred soldiers, a hundred workmen,
a hundred poor persons, with some number of widows, and many guests beside.'*

Lifris

Certain Welsh writings connect Cattwg with the court of King Arthur
and assert that he was one of its 'three knights of upright judgement, a
wise councillor, a wise bard, and one of the three knights who kept the
Holy Grail'. The following are a few examples of some of the wise sayings
attributed to Cattwg; many of them still make a great deal of sense in the
twentieth century:

'No one knows less than he who knows everything.'
'The best sorrow is sorrow for sin; and the best disposition is humility.'
'The service of divine religion I will never forsake for the allurements
    of the deceitful world, nor will I prefer earthly to heavenly things,
    neither will I despise what is eternal for what is momentary.'
'No one is discreet but he that perceives himself to be simple:
No one is knowing but he that knows himself:
No one is mighty but he that conquers himself:
No one is sensible but he that is aware of his misconception:
No one is wise but he that understands his ignorance:
No one is watchful but he that watches over himself:
No one is wary but he that avoids what his desire craves for:
No one is blind but he that sees not his own fault:
No one is discerning but he that discerns his own failing:
No one is strong but he that overcomes his own weakness.'

There is a certain mystery concerning the death and final burial place of
Cattwg, but, according to one story, he had a vision one night in which an
angel said to him 'choose the way in which you would like to die'. Cattwg
replied: 'I choose martyrdom.' The following day his monastery was raided

by pagans and Cattwg was pierced with a spear. Before he died he cried out to God: 'Help the Christians who dwell in my monasteries.'

It is quite likely that he was buried here at Llancarfan but it is of interest that an inscribed memorial stone bearing his name was discovered many years ago at Llandefaelog fach church, near Brecon (see page 106).

In 987 A.D. the monastery at Llancarfan was attacked by Danish invaders and it subsequently went into decline. A Tudor mansion was later constructed on the site and in the nineteenth century it became a farmhouse now known as Llanveithin, which has been variously spelt Llandoyeutha, Llantmeuthen, Llanvythin and Llanvathan. Many skeletons have been dug up in the garden where the burial ground of the old monastery was probably sited. About one hundred years ago some workmen were fitting a new window and in the thickness of the wall they discovered a skeleton which was later estimated to be over one thousand years old:

'The skull was covered with the most brilliant red hair and on examining the rest of the skeleton it was found that one leg had been cut off just below the knee. Around the skeleton lay little heaps of grey dust believed to be remnants of his clothes, and where one leg-bone had rested was a shoe.'

It is of interest that there is a tradition handed down from remote times that a Welshman was concealed in one of the thick walls of the monastery. He was said to have been a prince and a general who had been defeated in a battle fought in North Wales and was being pursued. Having previously been a student at the monastery he fled here for protection. It has been suggested that he was the bard Aneurin Gwawdrydd (the golden one of the free song) and the author of the seventh-century epic poem 'Y Gododin'. In this poem the battle of Cattraeth, which was fought in Scotland in 603 A.D. and at which Aneurin was reputed to be present, is described.

After being hidden at the monastery for some time a monk, who is said to have been either a great friend or a relation of a man that Aneurin had killed in battle, picked a quarrel with him and attacked him with a hatchet. He cut off the bard's leg and in consequence he bled to death. To conceal the murder, the body was hidden in the thick wall of the monastery.

At the time of the Norman Conquest, Llancarfan was taken over by Blondel de Mapes who married the daughter of its Welsh Lord. Their son was Walter de Mapes who became Archdeacon of Oxford and chaplain to Henry I. As a young man he translated the 'Brut y Brenhindedd' (The Chronicle of the Kings) from Welsh into Latin. Later in life, he translated the Latin version back into Welsh and inserted additional material of his own.

Bangor-is-y-Coed ('The Monastery under the Wood') Grid Reference unknown

In the Dark Ages a large and important religious settlement was founded here as a missionary seminary in the second century. It was converted into a monastery in about the year 530 A.D. by Cynwyl or Congela, the first abbot. In the Welsh Triads it is said to have contained 2400 monks, who in groups of 100 took turns to read prayers and sing psalms continually, so that divine service was performed unceasingly, day and night.

Nennius, a monk well known for his writings in the ninth century, subsequently became abbot of this monastery. The monastery was celebrated for its extensive library, and it flourished until 607 A.D. when Ethelfrid, King of Bernicia, attacked the settlement and murdered 1200 of the monks. They were slain because they were praying for the success of their countrymen in their battles against Ethelfrid.

The survivors fled to Bardsey Island (Ynys Enlli) which later became known as the Isle of the Saints (see page 175). Not the slightest trace of Bangor-is-y-Coed remains, but there is a location near Bangor on Dee which is known as Monk's Marsh.

Caerwent, between Newport and Chepstow, A48, Gwent ST 468905 (171)

Christianity was brought to Caerwent in the sixth century by Tatheus (Tathan), the only son of Tathalius, a king of Ireland. He was instructed in a vision 'to cross the water to Britannia', and so he sailed across the sea with seven of his followers. They landed at Portskewett (near Caerwent) and were hospitably received by King Ynyr, the son of Caradwg, who lived at the old Roman fort of Caerwent with his wife Madrun. Land was given to Tatheus to establish a church and in due course the community of Caerwent grew under his direction into an important centre of learning. One of his better-known disciples was Cattwg, who later founded his own monastery at Llancarfan.

The church of Tathan is believed to have stood near the north-east corner of the Roman fort. Excavations some years ago revealed the foundations of a building nearly square in shape with the apse turned towards the west.

In 1912, in an orchard of the vicarage, outside the walls of the Roman town, a stone coffin was dug up containing the bones of a human skeleton, thought to be Tathan himself. The coffin containing his bones was transferred to the present-day Caerwent church and laid below the floor of the south aisle. A slab bearing a Latin inscription was laid above the supposed remains:

'Here lies reverently, buried and enclosed in their original coffin, bones found in the orchard of the vicar of this parish, within the land on which about A.D. 560, St Tathan, under the benefaction of King Caradog, founded a church and college in honour of the Holy Trinity; in which church it is known that he and St Maches the virgin were buried; and so it is possible that these bones are the remains of that holy man. In memory whereof this stone was placed in A.D. 1912.'

Alternatively, Tathan is said to be the son of Amwn Ddu and his mother was Anna, a daughter of Meurig the son of Tewdrig, and some say that he lies buried at the Church of St Athan (Llandathan) in the Vale of Glamorgan.

Some of the other important seats of learning established during this period were as follows:

Bangor Tŷ Gwyn a Dav – The college of the White House on the Dav – which is the present Whitland Abbey in Dyfed, founded by Paul Hen or Paulinus in about 480 A.D..

Bangor Padarn – The college of Padarn – which was established at Llanbadarn Fawr near Aberystwyth by Padar, the son of Pedredin ap Emyr Llydaw, at the end of the fifth century.

Bangor Deiniol – The college of Deiniol – the son of Dunod ap Pabo, which was founded in 525 A.D.. It later became known as Bangor Fawr and was subsequently abbreviated to Bangor.

Côr Penmon was founded by Einion at the beginning of the sixth century. He placed Seiriol in charge of the institution that was subsequently called Côr Seiriol – the congregation of Seiriol.

Bangor Asaf – The college of Asaf – was later called Llan Elfy and in more recent times St Asaph. This was founded by Asaf under the direction of Cyndeyrn (Kentigern).

Côr Beuno – The congregation of Beuno – became Bangor Clynnog or the college of Clynnog and it is now known as Clynnog fawr.

Clynnog fawr, A499, south-west of Caernarvon, Gwynedd SH 414497 (115)

In the sixth century St Beuno founded a church here on land given to him by Cadwallon, king of Gwynedd. The present-day church is of much interest. There is a narrow passage about 15 feet long at the south-west side which leads to a small chapel called Eglwys y bedd. Some years ago, beneath the floor of this chapel, the remains of a small rectangular drystone building were found. There was a row of thirteen burials at its external west end and an empty slab cist outside the south wall. It would seem that the later church was built to cover the founder's church, part of the

160

original cemetery, and probably the grave of Beuno himself. His remains were subsequently moved to a new tomb in Eglwys y bedd.

There is an ancient stone in this church which is associated with St Beuno. It is 4 feet high and bears an inscribed cross which the saint is said to have traced with his thumb.

According to the *Llyfr Ancr* (Book of Anchorite), written at Llanddewi Brefi in 1346, Beuno was the son of Hywgi, or Bugi ap Gwynlliw Filwr, and Perferen, daughter of Llawdden Lwyddog of Dinas Eiddin. He has churches dedicated to him in most parts of Wales, and it has been said that there are more churches dedicated to Beuno in North Wales than to any other saint. Llanfeuno in south-western Herefordshire is the most southerly church dedicated to him in an area that was once part of Wales (see page 85).

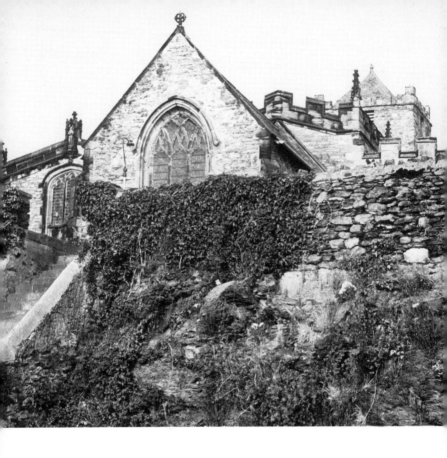

St Cybi's Church, Holyhead, Anglesey, Gwynedd SH 247827 (114)

This church stands in the middle of a fortress built by the Romans. In places the surrounding walls are 16 feet high and 6 feet thick, and they enclose a quadrangle 220 feet by 130 feet. The walls are constructed by unshaped blocks of granite that have been rounded by the wind and the rain over the centuries. Long after the Romans departed, the fortress was held by the Irish who were eventually evicted and defeated by Caswallon 'Long Hand' after a hard battle (see page 63). The fort later became a Royal Caer and was occasionally occupied in the sixth century by Maelgwyn Gwynedd, but he in due course gave it to St Cybi for the establishment of a church.

The present church stands on the site of the original structure erected by Cybi, and in the south doorway is a small effigy erected in his honour.

Llanbadrig, north Anglesey, off A5025, Gwynedd SH 375946 (114)

It is claimed locally that this church was founded by St Patrick. However, he was not the Irish patron saint but a namesake who lived later and was a member of St Cybi's monastery at Holyhead. The story is that he was returning from a visit to St Columba on Iona (Scotland) when his small boat was wrecked on Ynys Badrig. He swam ashore and scrambled up a rock, leaving the marks of his feet upon it. He later built a church here on the edge of the cliff to commemorate his escape from the clutches of the sea.

A strange feature at this site is the stone archway forming an entrance to the churchyard. It is said to be over 1000 years old.

St Trillo's Chapel, Rhos-on-Sea, Gwynedd SH 842812 (116)

On the edge of the sea near the promenade stands an ancient stone chapel, measuring 11 feet by 8 feet, which is said to have been founded by St Trillo in the sixth century. Inside is a holy well which was once famous for its healing powers. St Trillo is believed to have lived here for many years. He was the son of Hael of Llydaw and a brother of St Tegai and St Lleched.

The chapel is unlocked daily and is available for meditation and prayer or for inspection.

Capel Gwladys, near Cefn Gelligaer, Mid Glamorgan ST 125993 (171)

On a spur of open moorland the site of this sixth-century chapel, dedicated to St Gwladys, was discovered in 1906, not far from Hole Adam, a Roman road. A low stone wall has been erected to mark the site of the chapel and a stone replica of a Celtic cross of traditional design has been erected. This serves as a reminder that during the excavations a stone slab inscribed with a Celtic cross was found. It is now located in Gelligaer Parish Church a few miles away. This church is dedicated to Cattwg, the son of Gwladys, who was one of the many daughters of Brychan Brycheiniog.

St Cattwg is supposed to have been born at Bochriwcarn in the old parish of Gelligaer. In 546 he went to live in Brittany to avoid the plague which was sweeping through Britain at that time. In Brittany there are several churches dedicated to him and it is of interest that a painting of St Cattwg's church in Gelligaer can be seen in the Chapelle on the Ile de Cado in Brittany.

Llangendeirne Church, south-east of Carmarthen, Dyfed SN 455140 (159)

A strange discovery was made here in the nineteenth century when the church was being restored. Beneath the floor were found the skeletons of 497 men laid in layers five deep and closely packed. They had apparently been buried in tiers at the same time. Only adult male skeletons were found, and there were no signs of wounds on the limbs or skulls.

The church is dedicated to St Kentigern who spent some years in Wales when driven from his church in Scotland. There may have been a monastery here once, founded by the saint, and the remains could be those of his monks who died of yellow fever in 547.

Ogof Gwyl Edi (The Cave of St Eddy), off A483, south of Ammanford, Dyfed SN 591064 (159)

In the valley below Llanedy church, half concealed by bushes on an outcrop of rock, is a small cave which St Eddy is supposed to have used as a hermitage in the sixth century. They say that his bed and his seat can be seen in the shape of the rock inside the cave.

Pennant Melangell Church, off B4391, near Llangynog, Berwyn Mountains, south-east of Bala, Powys SJ 024265 (125)

St Monacella (Melangell) came to this peaceful valley in the eighth century and founded a primitive church. There is a square room at the end of the present church which is called Cell y Bedd (The Cell of the Grave) and this is her traditional burial place. It contains a reconstructed twelfth-century shrine. St Monacella is supposed to have been the daughter of Cyfwlch Addwyn (who was descended from Macsen Wledig), and she fled from his court to avoid an unwelcome marriage.

A story is told of the time when Brochwel Ysgythrog, Prince of the Powys, was out hunting hares one day when he came to a great thicket where he was amazed to find a virgin of surprising beauty, engaged in deep devotion. The hare that he had been following was sitting under her robe, boldly facing the dogs, who were sitting some distance away, howling their heads off. Brochwel was impressed with the holy lady and gave her land on which to build a church.

St Degan's Chapel, west of Trehowell, near Fishguard, Dyfed SM 889406 (157)

To the west of Trehowell in the Strumble Head area, near the edge of the cliffs and above a small creek, are the scanty remains of a small chapel dedicated to St Degan (or Dagan). It is claimed that the saint's habit was preserved there for 1100 years before being sold to a passing traveller in the eighteenth century.

Fenton, in his *Historical Tour through Pembrokeshire* of 1811, quotes from a letter written by H. Goff, a member of the Cathedral of St Davids:

'Above a small creek is a ruined chapel called St Degan's having near it a spring named after the saint; and above the spring a tumulus called St Degan's knoll where people resort to seat themselves on holidays and Sundays. There is a remarkable habit of this said St Degan preserved for several ages; the person that has it now having had it in his custody for forty years, to whom it was handed down by an elderly matron of upwards of ninety years of age. This habit, a piece whereof I have sent you enclosed, I had the curiosity to see; it is much in the form of a clergyman's cassock, but without sleeves. There are two of them of the same make, near a yard in length, but having the slit or hole at every corner on each end, and on the brim of each side were loops of blue silk.'

Fenton then gave the following information about St Degan:

'The veneration for this little duodecimo saint is hereditary amongst the inhabitants of this district, who tell a thousand miraculous tales of him and never fail to point out the prints of his horse's feet in the cliffs up which he rode when he emerged from the ocean, for it seems that he was a sort of marine production. Numerous prophecies likewise ascribed to him have been handed down from father to son for generations.'

Llanidan Church, near Bryn Siencyn, ¾ mile off A4080, Anglesey SH 495669 (115)

Dedicated to St Aidan, a seventh-century bishop, this church was at one time quite large, but it is now partially ruined. It contains the Maen Morddwyd (The Thigh Stone), which vaguely resembles a human thigh. The stone was once reputed to walk during the night and return by the morning. If taken away from the church it had the ability to return under its own steam. Earl Hugh of Chester once invaded Anglesey and on hearing about the famous walking stone he decided to test the truth of the legend. Attaching chains to the stone and with another large stone as an anchor, he cast them into a whirlpool in the Menai Straits. The stone was back in position the next morning, inside the church. At some period the stone was cemented into the wall of the church which no doubt ensures that it walks no more.

Lanidan church also boasts a holy water stoup which is apparently never filled but never found to be empty.

The church, which at one time was linked with the Augustinian priory at Beddgelert, was once much larger. There is a detached arcade in the churchyard, which adds to the desolate and spooky atmosphere of this disused church.

St Cenau's Chapel, Llangenny, near Crickhowell, Powys SO 241179 (161)

St Cenau came to live in this quiet valley below the Sugar Loaf mountain in the fifth century. Her oratory was situated about 400 yards above the present church. Unfortunately, it was demolished in 1790 and no trace of it remains. An iron bell was discovered by a local farmer some years afterwards; this was perhaps used by the saint for calling her neighbours to prayers (see page 179)

St Cenau died on 8 October 490 A.D. and was buried in her oratory by her nephew St Cattwg. It is said that before she passed away she spoke to Cattwg and made the following prophecy:

'This is the place above all others blessed by me. Here my memory shall be perpetuated. My tomb will lie a long time unknown, until the coming of other people, who by my prayers I shall bring hither. Them I will protect and defend, and in this place shall the name of the Lord be blessed forever.'

These 'other people' have not come yet for St Cenau's tomb has never been found, but her memory is certainly perpetuated for the village that stands here today is named after her.

St Gover's Stone, Llanover Church, Gwent SO 318094 (161)

At Llanover church, a few miles from Abergavenny, a long narrow slab can be seen below the inner door of the porch. There is a crude cross carved on the stone and it has been suggested that this once covered the grave of St Gover, the founder of this church. A well in the grounds of Llanover house is called Ffynnon Over.

Holy Islands

The wandering saints seemed particularly fond of living on islands, especially in later life when they sought solitude and perhaps wished to escape from the pressures of fifth- or sixth-century life. It was necessary for the old Celtic monks to live lives of great austerity and undertake hard manual work, for in those times such an existence was regarded as an essential condition of physical health and a holy life.

When old age and weariness came upon them many of the Celtic holy men sought the solitude of an island hermitage where they could enjoy an unobstructed view across the sea to the setting sun and could devote the remainder of their lives to prayer and meditation and then die in peace.

Ynys Pyr (Caldey Island), south of Tenby, Dyfed SS 1496 (158)

St Dubricius set up the first monastery on Caldey Island and Piro was appointed as abbot. It would seem that he enjoyed a drink or two, and sometimes indulged in three or four. One night, in about 520 A.D., he had one too many and, returning to his cell in a state of drunkenness, he fell into the island well. When his fellow monks pulled him out, they found that he had drowned.

Samson was then appointed as Piro's successor. He tried in vain to stop the monks' drinking habits. Finally, defeated by problems of discipline, he left Caldey and retired with some of the more faithful monks to Stackpole. The monks took over an abandoned camp that can still be seen today, and Samson settled into a cave in the side of the headland overlooking the sea.

St Cwyfan's Church, near Aberffraw, Anglesey, Gwynedd SH 335683 (114)

Built in the centre of a small circular island only 100 feet across is a tiny church dedicated to St Cwyfan. The llan boundary is formed by the edges of the island itself.

S. SEIRIOL. STAINED GLASS, PENMON

Ynys Seriol, near Penmon, Anglesey, Gwynedd SH 652827 (114)

Half a mile in length, this island is named after Seriol who established a cell here in the sixth century. The foundations of three walls can be seen standing within an oval-shaped llan (enclosure). To the north are the sites of a group of rectangular cells which were probably once occupied by St Seriol's followers.

In later years the island became known as Priestholm (Priests' Island) because it was used as a retreat by the monks of Penmon. The modern name is Puffin Island, for it is now more popular with puffins than either saints or priests!

Ynys Enlli, at southern end of Lleyn Peninsula, Gwynedd SH 1221 (123)

More commonly known as Bardsey Island, the original name is derived from Fenlli, a Welsh prince. The first monastery was founded here in 516 A.D. by Cadfan who had previously established a church at Tywyn (see page 100). Nothing remains of the original building except for a portion of a tower which is sometimes referred to as the abbot's lodge. An Augustinian monastery, dedicated to St Mary, was built on the same site, near the middle of the island, in the thirteenth century.

In the seventh century, when the monks of Bangor Iscoed were massacred, 900 of the survivors fled to this holy isle for safety and were no doubt numbered among the 20,000 saints that are supposed to be buried on the island in unmarked graves.

Taking into account the sanctity of the island and the problems of reaching it, three pilgrimages to Bardsey used to be rated as equal to a pilgrimage to Rome.

St Tecla's Chapel, near Severn Bridge, Gwent ST 548899 (162)

On a rocky islet near the mouth of the Wye are the ruins of an ancient chapel that is reputed to have been founded originally in the fourth century. It is dedicated to St Tecla, the daughter of Requli of Gwynedd. She abandoned the splendour of her father's court and retired to this lonely rock to pray and meditate. Some Vikings landed on the island, however, and murdered her. The stone chapel was built at a later date.

The church of Llandegla in Clwyd is also dedicated to her and a well nearby once had a reputation for curing epilepsy, known locally as clwy Tecla (St Tecla's disease).

Ynys Tysilio, Church Island, near Menai Bridge, in Menai Straits, Anglesey, Gwynedd SH 552717 (114)

St Tysilio set up a small hermitage on this little island in the sixth century as a base for his missionary work on Anglesey. It is linked to the mainland by a narrow causeway, and the present building was built in the fifteenth century on the site of the original building.

St Tysilio was the grandson of St Pabo, who had a church at Llanabo. His father was Brochwel Ysgythrog and two of his cousins were St Asaf and St Deiniol. In later years he became Abbot of Meifod, and, eventually, he went to Brittany to establish a monastery at St Malo, where he died and was buried in the neighbouring church of St Suliac.

Llanddwyn Island, south end of Anglesey, Gwynedd SH 386627 (114)

On this tiny island can be seen the simple church of St Dwynen. She was said to be a daughter of Brychan, the king of Brycheiniog, and became the Welsh patron saint of lovers.

> *'Who watches in thy chair, fair*
> *Dwynwen, no sickness or gloom*
> *of mind shall go with him from*
> *Llanddwyn.'*

Dafydd ap Gwilym

Burry Holms, at the north end of Rhossili Bay, Gower, West Glamorgan SS 401925 (159)

On this small island are the remains of a small chapel known as the Hermitage of St Kenyd. A few miles away inside Llangenydd church is a Celtic tombstone which is said to be that of St Kenyd. He was the son of Gildas and also the founder of Senghenydd in Mid Glamorgan. His son Fili constructed a fort at Caer Fili from which the present-day castle and town of Caerphilli take their name.

Flat Holm (or the Isle of Echni), Bristol Channel, Avon

St Gildas came here in the sixth century and built a small chapel. While he was here he wrote *The Gospel of St Gildas* which he later presented to Cattwg; it was kept at Llancarfan Monastery. Saxon pirates paid a visit to the island and destroyed the chapel of Gildas, but the saint survived by hiding in a cleft in the rocks.

Gildas, who is famous as the author of *De Excidio* – 'The destruction of Britain' – spent his final days at the monastery of Rhuys in Brittany where he is buried behind the altar.

Gateholm, South Pembrokeshire

This tiny islet was first occupied in the third century. Excavations have revealed the foundations of 130 huts arranged end to end in rows around small courtyards. Finds included pottery, a coin of Carausius, and a ring-headed pin of Irish design.

Machynys

A monastery was established in 513 by St Piro on this islet in the estuary of the Loughor river. The name was originally Mynach ynys (Monk's Island), which has been reduced to its present form.

Ramsey Island, west of St Davids, Dyfed SM 7023 (157)

Once called Ynys Tyfanog (St Tyfanog's Island), there used to be two chapels here. One was dedicated to St Devanus (Tyfanog or Dyfnog) and the other to St Justinian. Tyfanog came here to end his days 'in insular solitude, giving it a reputation for sanctity that continued long after his time' (Fenton). Some years later Justinian, a native of Brittany, obeyed a heavenly command to withdraw from the world and set sail in a coracle to reach Ramsey where he lived as a hermit.

10.
The Bells!
The Bells!

'When the bell begins to toll,
Lord have mercy on the soul.'

Bede

Celtic hand bell discovered at St Cenau's Chapel site at Llangenny, Powys
(see page 171)

During the Middle Ages, the bell relics of the Celtic Christian church founders were highly revered, but unfortunately very few of these bells have survived.

Giraldus Cambrensis, in his *Itinerary through Wales* written in the late twelfth century, made the following comment concerning superstitions associated with the bells of the saints at that time:

'. . . both the laity and clergy in Ireland, Scotland, and Wales, held in such veneration certain portable bells that they were more afraid of swearing falsely by them than by the Gospels, because of some hidden and miraculous power with which they were gifted; and by the vengeance of the saint, to whom they were particularly pleasing, their despisers and transgressors were severely punished.'

Bells are mentioned in the lives of many of the early saints. For example, when St Gildas visited St Cattwg at Llancarfan in 527 A.D. he carried a small bell that he had obtained in Ireland. Cattwg took a liking to the bell and asked if he could have it, but Gildas refused to part with it, saying that he wished to take the bell to Rome. In due course he arrived in Rome and showed his bell to Pope Alexander. However, it would not make any sound. The Pope then asked Gildas who was the last person to make the bell ring. When he was told that Cattwg had held it the Pope commented:

'The man of whom thou speakest was once known to me, for he journeyed hither seven times . . . for the remission of the souls of his parents and kinsfolk. This bell blessed by me and consecrated, carry back to the blessed Cattwg . . . Thus for two reasons will all the Britons reverence this bell, because it is blessed by me, and because it is owned by St Cattwg.'

Gildas, on his return, gave the bell to Cattwg who used it in his monastery at Llancarfan.

In the *Liber Landavensis* (The Book of Llandaff) we are informed that St Teilo was presented with a bell by his followers:

'that was more famous than great, more valuable in reality than appearance, because it exceeded every organ in sweetness of sound; it condemned the perjured, it healed the sick, and what appeared most wonderful, it sounded every hour without anyone moving it until being prevented by the sin of men, who rashly handling it with polluted hands, it ceased from such performance.'

Another interesting legend concerns the bell of St Oudoceus, the second Bishop of Llandaff:

> '*St Oudoceus being thirsty after undergoing labour, and more accustomed to drink water than any other liquor, came to a fountain in the Vale of Llandaff, not far from the church, that he might drink, where he found women washing butter, after the manner of the country, and sending them to his messengers and disciples, they requested that they would accommodate them with a vessel that their pastor might drink therefrom; who, ironically, as mischievous girls, said, "We have no other cup besides that which we hold in our hands," namely the butter; and the man of blessed memory taking it, formed one in the shape of a small bell, and he drank. And it remained in that form, that is, a golden one, so that it appeared to those who beheld it, to consist altogether of the purest gold; which by divine power is from that day reverently preserved in the church of Llandaff, in memory of the holy man, and it is said that by touching it, health is given to the diseased.*'

In his *Antiquitates Parochiales*, Rowland Rowland mentions a certain copper bell of an unusual shape called 'Cloch Velen Veuno', or the yellow bell of St Beuno, which in his time was preserved in the parish of Llanidan, Anglesey, and was said to have come from the ruins of a building called Capel Beuno. This relic has since disappeared, however.

Bede recorded that bells were used to summon the congregation to service, and so great was the fame of bells in this country that it was once known as the 'ringing island'.

The bell of the Celtic saint was quadrangular in form and about the same size and shape as an Alpine cowbell. The earliest ones were made of sheet iron dipped in molten bronze, but later they were cast in solid bronze. In superstitious times, bells were regarded as very sacred. They kept Satan away and prevented him from doing evil to the congregation.

Glascwm Church, between Builth Wells and Gladestry, Powys SN 155533 (148)

This little church is reputed to have been founded by St David in the sixth century. A bell called Bangu, said to be endowed with secret powers, was once kept here.

Trevethin Church, near Pontypool, Gwent ST 283020 (171)

In the church of St Cadoc (Cattwg) at Trevethin, they say that there used to be a bell with amazing powers. It was a gift to the church from Llywelyn ap Iorwerth, Lord of Caerleon. One day a child climbed into the belfry and was struck dead by the bell. The people of the parish were so upset by the incident that they took the bell away and buried it. Ever since that day, it is said that when a child in this parish is accidentally killed the bell of St Cadoc can be heard tolling mournfully beneath the ground.

Dolwyddelan Church, now on A470, north of Blaenau Ffestiniog, Gwynedd SH 735524 (115)

One of the treasures of this little church in the Lledr valley is the Cloch Wyddelan or Gwyddelan's bell, which many years ago was dug up on the site of the old church at Bryn y Bedd. It is made of cast bronze, or possibly sheet metal dipped in bronze, and it retains its original brass handle. The bell measures 8¾ inches in height and is oval in plan, measuring 8¾ inches by 6¼ inches at the base and at the top 6 inches by 3 inches.

It was probably a bell of this type, made of brass or copper sheet metal and covered in molten metal, that Gildas gave to St David in the sixth century and which he in turn gave to St Illtud (see *Mysterious Wales*). Other Celtic handbells have been discovered at the following church sites:

Llangwynadl (Gwynedd)	Cast bronze handbell
Llanrhyddlad (Gwynedd)	Cast bronze handbell
Llangystenyn (Gwynedd)	Cast bronze handbell
Llangennau (Powys)	Iron handbell
Newcastle, Bridgend (Glamorgan)	Iron handbell

 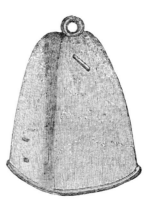

Llanwynno Church, in the Forest of St Gwynno, to the north-west of Pontypridd, Mid Glamorgan SS 030957 (170)

Long ago the church bell was stolen from Llanwynno and hidden on the hillside near the source of the Ffrwyd. The spot is still called Ffos y Gloch – The Ditch of the Bell. Apparently, the thieves were unable to carry it away that night so they buried it in the peaty soil. Later they returned and dug up the bell, taking it away on a sledge under the cover of darkness. But when they were crossing the Clydach (at a spot later called Rhyd y Gloch – The Ford of the Bell), near Cwm Clydach, the sledge shook wildly and the bell rang with a loud clang, alerting the local people who chased after the thieves. They caught up with them in a valley the other side of Merthyr Mountain at Rhyd y Car – The Ford of the Sledge.

Site of Rhyader Castle, Powys SN 970678 (147)

In the twelfth century a certain knight was imprisoned in the castle of Rhyader. His wife being a good Catholic and devoted to him sought the aid of the monks to help him escape. After some discussion the monks provided her with a magic bell, which possessed the power of liberating from confinement any prisoner who should set it up on the wall and ring it. The woman succeeded in getting the bell secretly into her husband's prison and he set it up on the wall and promptly rang it. But although he had gathered together his possessions and was fully prepared to leave, the doors of his prison refused to open.

Shortly afterwards the castle was struck by lightning and both it and the town were burned in one night, except for the wall upon which the magic bell was hanging. Today, nothing remains of the castle at all.

Whitesands Bay, near St Davids, Dyfed SM 733265 (157)

There is a local legend that the largest bell of St Davids Cathedral was once carried away by evil forces and buried in Whitesands Bay. The bell is supposed to be heard tolling a warning when a storm is brewing, and local fishermen used to listen for it as an omen of bad weather.

The Bells of Aberdovey, A493, Gwynedd SN 615960 (135)

This popular seaside resort has been made famous by the song 'The Bells of Aberdovey', which is based on a legend concerning a church that was buried below the water when the sea engulfed the lower part of Aberdovey. It is said that the bells can be heard ringing on calm nights. Sometimes a single bell is heard and at other times the complete carillon. The song was composed by Dibdin for the opera *Liberty Hall*, which was first performed at Drury Lane Theatre in 1785.

11.
Holy Wells
and their Cures

'There are in Wales wells which must have been sacred even in pre-Christian times, wells transformed from pagan to Christian usages, and wells that claim a purely Christian origin. Legends, practices, beliefs and folktales, the accretions of centuries, encrust them, with the result that their original significance has been obscured.'

Francis Jones, *The Holy Wells of Wales*

St Non's Well, near St Davids, Dyfed

In most parishes in Wales there is at least one holy well to be found, generally bearing the name of the saint who founded the nearby church, or to whomever it was later dedicated.

A comprehensive survey of holy wells in Wales was undertaken by Francis Jones, who in 1950 published his findings in a book entitled *The Holy Wells of Wales*. He identified a total of 1179 wells and found that 437 of them were named after saints and 369 were said to possess healing properties.

To some was attributed the power of healing all bodily diseases known, but the majority were renowned for providing a remedy for a particular ailment. Others were accredited with the power of bringing good fortune. People once took these matters very seriously and travelled great distances in order to visit the appropriate well either to be cured of their complaint, or in the hope of bringing about some change in their luck and future prosperity.

It was of course most important to select the appropriate well for your particular complaint. The following list provides a general guide for a wide variety of ailments:

Inflamed eyes	Chapel Well, near Usk, Gwent
Inflammations, ulcers, warts	Llantilio Pertholey, Gwent
Infantile ailments	Ffynnon Isel, Hirnant Parish, Powys
Ague and intestinal complaints	Ffynnon Canna, Llangan, Dyfed
Tuberculosis, whooping cough	Ffynnon Deilo, Dyfed
Failing eyesight	St Govan's Well, Bosherton, Dyfed
Weak sinews	Pistyll Goleu, Dyfed
Scabs, ulcers, rickets	Job's Well, Carmarthen, Dyfed
Sprains	Ffynnon Bedr, Dyfed
Pox	Ffynnon Ddyfnog, Dyfed
Epilepsy	Ffynnon Degla, Clwyd
Nervous complaints	Ffynnon Asa, Clwyd
Pains in the head	Ffynnon Barruc, Barry Island, South Glamorgan
Gout and all aches	Llangynwydd Well, Glamorgan
Bowel complaints	Ffynnon Gwylliad, Bwlch y Groes, Gwynedd

Gangrene	Ffynnon Bedrog, Llanbedrog, Gwynedd
Rickets	Ffynnon Beris, Nant Peris, Gwynedd
All ills!	Ffynnon Cawrdaf, Gwynedd
Blindness	Ffynnon Gybi, Llangybi, Gwynedd
Malignant ulcers	Ffynnon Saethau, Llanfihangel Bachellaeth, Gwynedd
Sterility in women	Ffynnon y Brenin, Llaniestyn, Gwynedd
Wounds and sores	Ffynnon Trisant, Devil's Bridge, Dyfed
Diarrhoea	Ffynnon Lwli, Llangynllo, Dyfed
Lumbago	Ffynnon Pistyll Cynwy, Llangynllo parish, Dyfed
Blindness	Ffynnon Francis, Llanfihangel Genau'r-glyn, Dyfed
Hair restoration	Marcross Well, Dyfed
Feminine complaints	Holywell, Clwyd
	Ffynnon y Filiast, Dyfed
	Ffynnon y Brenin, Dyfed
Alcoholism	Ffynnon Barruc, Barry Island, South Glamorgan
Rheumatism and lameness	Taff's Well, near Cardiff, South Glamorgan

Well rituals

A variety of rituals had to be observed at the chosen well, in order to ensure the cure. Sometimes, they were quite simple, like the following examples:
Drink from the palm of your hand (Ffynnon Aaran, Dyfed)
Drink from a limpet shell (Ffynnon Govan, Dyfed)
Drink from a skull (Ffynnon Teilo, Dyfed)

After drinking from the well, sleep on a nearby stone.
For example, Coed y ffynnon (Penmachno, Gwynedd) where one slept afterwards on Carreg y Ddefod (Stone of the Rite).

Throw a bent pin or a brass buckle into the well, then silently pray, then wish and then travel home without speaking to anyone. (Ffynnon Barruc, South Glamorgan)

Carry a candle and wish for a cure. (St Dwynwyn's Well, Anglesey)
Recite the Lord's Prayer. (Penginger Well, Brecon, Powys)

Make the sign of the cross. (Ffynnon y Groes, Dyfed)

Utter the following words: (Ffynnon Fair Rhaedr, Glamorgan)
Frimpanfroo, Frimpanfroo
Sali Bwli la
iri a.

The rituals were sometimes more involved and wellkeepers gave those seeking a cure written instructions on the payment of a sum of money.

At Ffynnon Degla (Clwyd), if seeking a cure for epilepsy or mental disorder, the patient should act as follows:

1. Visit the well after sunset on a Friday.
2. Wash hands and feet in the well.
3. Walk around the well three times carrying a cock in a basket.
4. Prick the cock with a pin and throw the pin in the well.
5. Give a groat at the well to the parish clerk.
6. Walk around Llandegla church three times reciting the Lord's Prayer.
7. Enter the church and place a groat in the Poor Box.
8. Lie under the Communion Table until daybreak with the church Bible as a pillow and covered with a carpet.
9. Transfer the disease by placing the cock's beak in your mouth. Blow into it and then let the bird go.
10. Put a piece of silver in the Poor Box.
11. Leave the cock in the church; if it dies, you are cured.

St Govan's Well, near St Govan's Chapel, south of Pembroke, Dyfed SS 967929 (158)

This little stone-covered well is situated directly below the chapel of St Govan, built in a cleft between the limestone cliffs. It is now dry, but at one time it was visited regularly by people seeking a cure for lameness, many of them travelling from remote parts of Wales to bathe their limbs in the holy water. It would appear that for some the trip was worthwhile, for in 1811 Richard Fenton recorded in his *Historical Tour through Pembrokeshire* that there were many crutches left here by people who had been healed.

St Illtud's Well, near Llanrhidian Church, Gower, West Glamorgan SS 497923 (159)

According to the Annals of Margam of 1185, this well, at certain times of the year for a period of three hours on Thursdays, flows with milk instead of water.

Ffynnon Gloch, near Llanarth, Dyfed SN 423577 (146)

Near the church is Ffynnon Gloch, which is said to be under a spell. People standing here are unable to hear the church bells when they are ringing. A local legend recalls how the Devil stole a bell from Llanbadarn Fawr church and rested near this well which then became cursed.

Ffynnon Gwynwg, near Llangelnin Church, Gwynedd SH 571072 (124)

Here is a well that is said to specialize in healing warts. If anyone wished to be rid of a wart the answer was to throw a bent pin into the well and the wart would soon disappear. It is said that about one hundred years ago the bottom of the well was covered with pins and that people were always careful not to touch them, fearing that the warts deposited with the pins would grow on their own hands if they did so.

The Wells of the Two Saints, near Llanerchymedd, Anglesey, Gwynedd SH 401828 (114)

There used to be two wells near this village, named after St Cybi and St Seiriol who developed the habit of meeting here at midday. Cybi walked here from the west and Seiriol came from his habitation in the east. Cybi would make an early start, walking the old Roman road, and he had the sun shining on his face all the way. His friend Seiriol made his journey with the sun at his back. They met at noon, had lunch and drank from their respective wells. Cybi then retraced his steps to the west and Seiriol went home to the east. Consequently, Cybi had the evening sun shining on his face for his homeward stroll, while Seiriol walked with his shadow before him. It would seem that Cybi always looked well tanned and Seiriol remained pale. They became known as Cybi the tawny and Seiriol the fair.

Ffynnon Canna, near Llangain Church, Dyfed SN 389156 (159)

Visitors to this well seeking a cure offered a pin to the water and then drank or bathed. They then left the well and followed a path into a field adjoining the church where a strange stone resembling a chair can be seen. The sick person would then sit in the stone 'chair' and, if he or she managed to sleep in this uncomfortable position, then the holy water from the well was sure to cure them. The process was usually repeated over a period of several days, and very often over a period of two or three weeks if the person was particularly determined to obtain a cure.

Ffynnon Garedig, Dyfed

In the parish of Llanllwni this well was once famous for testing a person's health. By holding your arms in the well for a certain length of time, so it was said, you may find out if you are sick or well. If your arms are red when you take them out of the water, it is believed to be a sign of good health; if they are white then you are not well, so the legend went, and should see a doctor.

St Teilo's Well, near the ruined church of Llandilio, near Maenchlochog, Dyfed SN 104272 (145)

The Melchior family used to be the traditional custodians of this well which had a local reputation for healing chest complaints. Sufferers used to come here and drink the water from a human cranium which was said to be part of St Teilo's skull.

A large flat stone beside the well apparently used to ring when struck and would continue ringing until the holy water was taken inside the church. The stone was eventually broken up, for it frightened passing horses.

Ffynnon Gellionen in South Glamorgan

This is a well that was said to be able to control the local weather. It was visited during periods of drought and the waters were sprinkled around to induce rain to fall. People then danced around and threw flowers to one another and sang Welsh ballads. They then cried out three times 'Bring us rain!' and filled containers with the well water and sprinkled it on their gardens.

Llanllawer Well, near Llanllawer Church, south-east of Fishguard, Dyfed SM 986359 (157)

This recently restored well in a field near Llanllawer church once had the reputation of possessing medicinal properties and was much frequented in earlier times.

The Well at World's End, near Eglwyseg, north of Llangollen,
Clwyd SJ 234476 (117)

A spring of cold water is situated halfway down the steep gorge between
Craig Aderyn and Craig y Forwyn. In winter, it can be very remote and
desolate below the Eglwyseg rocks which tower above the gorge. It is
undoubtedly a place with a magical atmosphere shrouded in romance and
mystery.

'I came to the place of rocks which forms the uttermost limits of the valley. Some of the rocks were livid, some were grey, and some, in the bed of the stream, were of the colour of ancient bloodstains. The voice of the stream echoed through all this place in a continuous and loud lament. I sat there for a space, and noted how that voice never varied its utterance, and yet in spite of that, it was now like the clamour of armed men, and now like two voices speaking together, the one pleadingly, the other mockingly.'

Dixon Scott

Ffynnon Cybi (St Cybi's Well), Llangybi, north-east of Pwllheli, Gwynedd SH 429412 (123)

Ffynnon Cybi, near the church, is famous for its healing powers and the ability to inform maidens of their lovers' faithfulness. A rag would be thrown on to the water. If it floated south, everything would be fine, but if it went to the north, the girl would be unhappy.

St Cybi and his uncle Cyngar with a band of disciples crossed the Irish Sea in a large coracle and were shipwrecked near here in the sixth century. Cybi later built a small sanctuary and settled here for many years. One day Prince Maelgwyn Gwynedd was hunting in the area and a goat that he was pursuing ran to St Cybi for protection. The prince followed the goat and on meeting the holy man was very impressed and promised him some land on which to build a church. He asked Cybi how much land he would like. The saint replied that he would like as much land as the hounds could cover before catching the goat. On releasing the goat, it led the hounds around the entire peninsula of Lleyn and back to St Cybi – much to the Prince's amazement.

St. Cybi's Well, Carnarvonshire.

193

Ffynnon Beuno (St Beuno's Well), Clynnog, Lleyn Peninsula, Gwynedd SH 413495 (115)

Now beside the A499, just west of Clynnog church, is St Beuno's Well which was conveniently sited for pilgrims making their way to Bardsey Island. The water in the well was once believed to be a sure cure for blindness, especially if scrapings from the pillars of St Beuno's chapel (in Clynnog Church) were dissolved in it.

Another custom held that sick people should first bathe in the well and then go to sleep on a tombstone covered in rushes, inside Capel Beuno. When Pennant, the historian, came here in the eighteenth century, he observed on this stone 'a feather bed, on which a poor paralytic from Merionethshire had lain the whole night'. It was believed that if the person slept then the cure would be successful.

People from far and wide used to bring their children to be healed of ailments, and they paid an annual tribute to Beuno's Chest (Cyff Beuno) to ensure the prosperity of their sheep and cattle.

St Seiriol's Well, Penmon, Anglesey SH 630807 (115)

Two hundred yards north-east of Penmon Priory church is a stone structure enclosing a well. Nearby are the foundations of a raised hut where St Seiriol is supposed to have lived.

St John's Well, Newton, near Porthcawl, West Glamorgan SS
839774 (170)

Sometimes referred to as Sandford's Well, it is affected by the flow of the
sea which is ¼ mile away. When the tide is out the well is full, but when
the tide comes in the well is empty.

The novelist R. D. Blackmore, in his book *The Maid of Sker*, described
the well:

*'This well has puzzled all the country and all the men of great learning, being as full
of contrariety as a maiden courted. It comes and goes, in a manner against the coming
and going of the sea, which is only half a mile from it; and twice a day it is many feet
deep and again not as many inches. And the water is so crystal clear that down in the
dark it is like a dream.'*

Maen Du Well, near Brecon, Powys SO 039296 (160)

This ancient holy well is covered by a stone building that was reconstructed in 1754 and resembles a sixth-century Celtic chapel. At one time the well was used by lovers who first threw pins into the water and then earnestly wished for happiness.

Not all wells were used for healing purposes. Some were known as cursing wells and were visited in the hope of inflicting discomfort and even death on the unsuspecting victim. An example is Ffynnon Aelian near Bettws Abergeley, Clwyd.

'Near the well resided a woman who officiated as a kind of priestess. Anyone who wished to inflict a curse upon an enemy resorted to this priestess, and for a trifling sum she registered in a book kept for the purpose the name of the person on whom the curse was wished to fall. A pin was then dropped into the well in the name of the victim and the curse was complete.'

A. W. Gomme
Ethnology in Folklore

12.
Natural
Wonders

'Folklore collects and compares the remains of ancient people, superstitions and facts which survive, ideas which live in our time, but are not of our time.'

Andrew Lang
Custom and Myth

Lydstep Cavern, Dyfed

It was Nennius who in the ninth century first recorded some of the natural wonders of Wales in his fascinating manuscript entitled *History of the Britons*. A section near the end of his work deals with the 'Twenty Marvels of Britain'; some of the Welsh ones are of particular interest and can still be seen today, such as the Severn Bore which he describes in the following terms:

'Another miracle is that of the two kings of the Severn – when the sea overflows at high tide at the mouth of the Severn, two masses of foam are separately accumulated, and make war after the manner of two rams, and each attacks the other and they beat each other alternately. And again one retires from the other and they attack in one mass over all the face of the sea. In each tide they do this from the beginning of the world to this day.'

Over the centuries many more 'marvels' have been identified by other writers, such as Giraldus Cambrensis, who have provided fascinating explanations for the origin of natural curiosities and unusual features in the landscape.

The following are examples of the interesting places in Wales that have been regarded in times past with awe, and locations that the superstitious would certainly avoid visiting alone or in the dark.

Llyn Arenig, to the west of Bala, Gwynedd SJ 845380 (125)

An easy ascent along a well-defined track leads up to this lake from a layby on a road to the north of it at SJ 845395. The lake is beautifully situated below the lower craggy slopes of Arenig Fawr, and it is said that if the atmospheric conditions are favourable a strange echo may be heard here. It has been described as resembling 'an echo played on the keys of a piano'.

Penrhyn gŵyr (Worm's Head), near Rhossili, Gower, West Glamorgan SS 385877 (159)

Jutting dramatically into the sea at Rhossili, this impressive headland is the most westerly point of Gower and West Glamorgan. The causeway between the inner head and the mainland starts to be exposed to ebb tide about 2½ hours after high water, when it becomes possible to scramble across the rocks to reach the mile-long promontory. The inner and outer heads are connected by an arch of rock called the Devil's Bridge, and on the north side is a blowhole which emits a loud hissing and booming noise. Air is forced through a cleft in the rocks by waves pounding against the north side of the Worm and a handkerchief placed over the hole will be blown several feet into the air.

The sixteenth-century historian Leland described Worm's Head as follows:

'There is in Gowerland, bytwixt Swansey and Lochor a litle promontori caullid Wormes Hedde, from which to Caldey is communely caullid Sinus Tinbechicus . . . there is a wonderful hole at the poynt of Worms Heade, but few dare enter into it, and men fable that there is a dore witheien that spatius hole wich hathe be sene withe greate nayles on it.'

Warning: Check tides at coastguard office before venturing on to the Worm and do not leave it for the mainland later than 3½ hours before high tide.

The Green Bridge of Wales, near Elegug Stacks, 3 miles west of
Bosherton, Dyfed SR 925944 (158)

This magnificent rock arch is one of the best-known features of the
impressive coastal scenery in the Pembrokeshire National Park and is
much photographed by those who come here to walk the coastal path.

One local story about the arch concerns a shepherd who once, long ago,
discovered a secret passage near this romantic situation. On entering the
passage he found that:

*'in many places it was spacious and beautiful, abounding fountains and verdant
meads; but afraid to proceed without company further, he reluctantly returned. Some
weeks later, taking his faithful dog with him, he made a second expedition, but fell a
sacrifice to his curiosity, never being heard of more. That after many days waiting to
see if his master would awake, as they conjecture, the dog reduced for worse of food to
a mere skeleton, came out alive on the sea shore.'*

The Monk's Cave, 5 miles south of Aberystwyth, Dyfed SN 546746 (135)

An impressive collapsed sea cave that can only be reached by walking along the beach from Aberystwyth when the tide is going down. It is also known as Twll Twrw or the Thunder Hole, for, when the sea rushes into the cave during high spring tides and westerly gales, it sounds like thunder.

The Bellowing Cave, Barry Island, south-west of Cardiff, South Glamorgan ST 118662 (171)

Giraldus Cambrensis, the twelfth-century historian, came here on his tour of Wales in 1188 and recorded the following description of a blowhole that used to be regarded as one of the wonders of Wales:

'In a rock near the entrance to the island there is a small cavity, to which, if the ear is applied, a noise is heard like that of smiths at work, the blowing of bellows, strokes of hammers, grinding of tools and roaring of furnaces; and it might easily be imagined that such noises which are continued at the ebb and flow of the tides, were occasioned by the influx of the sea under the cavities of the rocks.'

There are numerous other blowholes on the cliffs of Wales and two more examples can be seen at the following locations:

Bosherton Mere, near St Govan's Chapel, Dyfed SM 962928 (158)

This remarkable blowhole was described by the historian Camden:

'Near Stackpole is Bosher, otherwise Bosherton. Upon the sea side is a pool or a pit called Bosherton Mere – the depth whereof several that have sounded have not yet discovered. The pit bubbles and foams, and makes such a noise before stormy weather that it is heard above ten miles away.'

Pwll y Gwynt, near Southerndown, West Glamorgan SS 882733 (170)

To the west of Dunraven, above Southerndown sands is another wind hole. As the sea thunders into a chamber far below, one hears a harsh rush of air and a loud rumbling noise. A handkerchief placed over the mouth of the hole will be blown several feet into the air.

The Whistling Sands, Porth Oer, 2 miles north of Aberdaron, Lleyn Peninsula, Gwynedd SH 167300 (123)

Porth Oer claims to have a remarkable beach where, in certain dry and atmospheric conditions, the sand makes a loud whistling noise when you walk across it.

Logans or Rocking Stones

These are large boulders, delicately balanced, which may be caused to rock when pushed gently in the appropriate direction. Eighteenth-century antiquaries maintained that these curiosities had been set in place by the Druids who used them as sacrificial altars or to demonstrate their magic powers.

Geologists would offer the explanation that they are natural rocks which have been weathered along the joints and become separated from the underlying rock on which they are now balanced. Alternatively, in glaciated areas they could be perched blocks which have been carried by ice and finally come to rest on another rock.

The Buckstone, near Staunton, Gwent SO 543123 (162)

Here can be seen the largest logan stone in Wales. It is a large mass of Conglomerate, and at one time it used to rock when pushed in the appropriate place. Unfortunately, it was overturned in 1885, and rolled down the hillside to break into three pieces. A few years later the fragments were dragged back up the slope and cemented together, but the boulder no longer rocks. The site is still well worth a visit, however, for it provides an excellent viewing point of the surrounding countryside.

Maen Sigl, Great Ormes Head, near Llandudno, Gwynedd SC 776835 (115)

To find this curious rocking stone, go up the Happy Valley and follow a path to Pen Dinas. The stone is perched on rocky ground overlooking the valley. It is sometimes referred to as Cryd Tudno (Tudno's Cradle) and measures 6 feet long by 2½ feet broad. A hefty push will make it rock.

Pennant came here in 1774 and wrote

'Near this place is Maen Sigl, rocking stone, a great one, whose point of contact with the ground is so small as to make it moveable with the least touch. The country people call it Cryd Tudno, St Tudno's Cradle. This is surrounded with a foss, and has a farmed road leading to it. It is the conjecture of the learned, that the Druids made these stones an instrument of the imposition of their votaries; and in case of any judicial determinations, pretended that none but their holy hands could move them: and probably they were surrounded with a foss, and had their prescribed road to keep off the vulgar, and give greater solemnity to their miraculous decision.'

William Morris came here in 1761 and wrote 'I touched it with my finger and it rocked.'

The Rocking Stone, Pontypridd Common, Mid Glamorgan ST 083902 (170)

Just opposite the Cottage Hospital, overlooking Pontypridd, is a huge block of sandstone which provides a good vantage point for the surrounding area. According to the Bard Iolo Morgannwg, this was the site of the original Gorsedd, or assembly of the Bards. Although it weighs about 9½ tons the rock can be made to vibrate at the touch of a child's finger and move quite violently at a push from an adult's hand pressing on its south side.

'The breeze-blown common on the top of a high hill overlooking the town is said to have been a burial place of the ancient Welsh Princes. There is a Druidical circle of stones up there . . . and a logan stone, upon which strange mysterious rites are performed in the face of the sun, on St John's Eve and other traditional anniversaries.'

Wirt Sikes, Rambles and Studies in Old South Wales

THE LOCAL SEA-MONSTER
An artist's impression of what the
schoolgirls saw entering the water
near Barmouth.

The Mawddach Monster, Barmouth, Gwynedd

Stories are told of a monster living in the Mawddach Estuary. Numerous people over the years have claimed to have seen it, including six schoolgirls who watched it in broad daylight on 2 March, 1975:

'It had a long neck and a square face and a long tail with a flipper at the back and its skin was black and patchy.'

A local woman once claimed to have seen four large footprints 'as big as an elephant's' on the wet sand near Barmouth. Another account came from Mr Jones of Harlech who, in 1937, observed a 'crocodile-like creature' walking beside a riverbank just outside the town. A shopkeeper in Barmouth (Mr Walter of High Street, Tyn y coed,) has mounted a display of newspaper cuttings and over the years has taken a special interest in the history of the monster's sightings.

It is a strange coincidence that the Barmouth coat-of-arms, which may be seen on the front of a building in High Street, shows the head of a monster, which is surely confirmation that sightings of the Mawddach Monster have become well established over many years.

The Monster of Moel Cynwch, near Dolgellau, Gwynedd SH 733204 (124)

Long ago a huge serpent terrorized this neighbourhood and anyone who was unfortunate enough to meet it and looked into its eyes would be paralysed and eaten.

The Lord of Nannau offered a reward of sixty cattle to anyone who could kill the monster, but no one was brave enough to take up the challenge. However, one day a shepherd came this way by chance and found the beast asleep. He killed it by driving a stake through its eye and buried the animal on the hillside. The burial site is still known as Carnedd Bedd y Wibr – 'The Grave of the Serpent'.

Teggy of Llyn Tegid (Bala Lake), Bala Gwynedd SJ 9134 (125) – grid reference of the Lake

This monster has been spotted regularly during the last twenty years and the individual descriptions coincide quite well. In 1983, one local man was looking down on the lake at about 10.00 A.M. when to his amazement he saw an object about 10 feet long moving slowly down towards the bank. He rushed down to the foreshore but the 'thing' had disappeared. A local fisherman suggested that it might have been two otters swimming one behind the other, but the man who saw the monster couldn't readily accept that explanation. He commented, 'I have seen and I know I have seen something on which I need an explanation and until I get that explanation, then the monster remains.'

Local people call the Bala monster Anghenfil; it has been seen regularly over the last fifteen years.

A local man was fishing one day in calm water on the edge of the lake when the creature rose up and came towards him. 'It had a large body – about 8 feet long – and a huge head with glaring eyes. Its skin was dark and shiny.' He watched for about thirty seconds before it disappeared into the water.

Llyn y Gadair, near Rhyd Ddu on the Caernarvon to Beddgelert Road, Gwynedd SH 5652 (115)

At one time a terrible golden-haired monster was supposed to live in a lair near this lake. It caused a great deal of mischief in the neighbourhood until it was eventually chased up the pass of Drwys y Coed and slain.

A tale is told of a man in the eighteenth century who swam across the lake and at the halfway point was seen to be followed by a long trailing object which, as he neared the shore, enveloped him in its great coils. To the horror of his friends watching on the bank, it dragged him into a deep hole at the mouth of a stream.

Llyn Gwyn Lake, south-west of Nantmel, near Rhyader, Powys SO 012648 (147)

This lake, about one mile in circumference, with its steep sloping sides, is reputed to be bottomless. Local people used to treat it with respect – even awe. A story is told of a man whose pony once carried him across its frozen surface in a snowstorm. He died of shock when he looked back and realized where he had ridden.

Llyn Glaslyn, below the east face of Snowdon, Gwynedd SH 615545 (115)

This lake was originally called Llyn Ffynnon Las (the lake of the Green Well). It has a sinister reputation and is reputed to be bottomless; it is haunted by a monster living in its depths. Previously, it is said, he lived in the Fairy Glen, a romantic ravine near the confluence of the Lledr and the Conwy. The monster was quite a problem in this area for he wandered around killing local people. So they sent for the magician Myrddin (Merlin) who put a spell on the beast. It was then caught by the giant Hu Gadarn and dragged across country to Snowdon by a team of white oxen.

They pulled it over the pass between Siabod and Cribau; hence the name Bwlch yr Ychain (Pass of the Oxen). The strain of crossing this pass was, apparently, so great that one of the oxen lost an eye on the western slopes. This spot was later called Gwaun Llygad yr Ych – 'The Field of the Ox's Eye' – and its tears formed a pool called Pwll Llygad yr Ych 'which never dries up, although no stream either enters it or flows out of it'. The expedition reached Llyn Glaslyn without any further incidents and the monster was thrown into the watery depths.

Shepherds in the early eighteenth century, who claimed to have seen the monster, described it as 'toadlike and with tails and wings'. They said that it also made horrible shrieking noises.

Llyn Dulyn (Black Pool), below Foel-grach, Carneddau Mountains, Gwynedd SH 700665 (115)

Llyn Dulyn is enclosed by 500-feet cliffs in a very wild and gloomy setting. The colour of the water appears black and sinister, as is indicated by the name of the lake.

Local shepherds used to say that the appearance of a dove near the water foretold the descent of a beautiful but wicked woman's soul to torment in the underworld. In the seventeenth century it was also believed that if anyone had the courage to watch beside Llyn Dulyn on a certain night, they would see who was to die within the next twelve months. Fiends would rise from the lake and drag those who had led evil lives into the deep waters. A witch once disappeared from the district and a shepherd claimed that he saw her being dragged into the lake.

Nash Sands, near St Donats, West Glamorgan SS 912690 (170)

Beware of Nash Sands 'because there is a winch in them'. This is a sort of bottomless whirlpool, into which if you should fall you will never be seen again. Swimmers were once warned against the 'winch' in Nash Passage, which was known as the Great Gutter. The waves that break around the dreaded Nash Point are called the Merry Dancers, and the souls of the drowned men were once thought to be holding revels among them.

River Taff near Cardiff, South Glamorgan. Grid reference unknown.

A whirlpool in the River Taff was once noted as one of the 'seven wonders of Glamorgan'. It apparently forms a small lake in times of drought when the riverbed is almost dry. Local folk used to claim that it was bottomless and that in its depths a monstrous serpent lived and fed upon the unfortunate victims that were drowned in the river and sucked into the whirlpool.

The Taff whirlpool was also said to be haunted by a beautiful lady who lured bathers to their doom. They swam towards her and were then sucked into the depths of the whirlpool; their bodies were never found. The evil lady was believed to be the Devil in disguise.

Llyn Crumlyn, south-west of Neath, West Glamorgan SS 703955 (170)

Situated in Crymlyn Bog, this lake is reputed to cover an ancient city, with magnificent buildings hidden in its depths. People say that on certain occasions strains of weird music can sometimes be heard floating up from the dark waters. Another pool in the bog is known as Pwll Conan (Conan's Pool) and is named after the grandson of Rhys ap Tewdwr, King of Dyfed, who was drowned here on his return from the battle of Hirwaun Wrgan in the eleventh century (see page 230).

13.
Hoards of
Buried Treasure

*'Vortigern left his treasure at Dinas Emrys. One day
a youth with yellow hair and blue eyes shall come.
When he steps on a spot above the cave, a bell will
ring and the cave will open of itself so that he may
have the treasure.'*

           T. Gwynn Jones, 1930

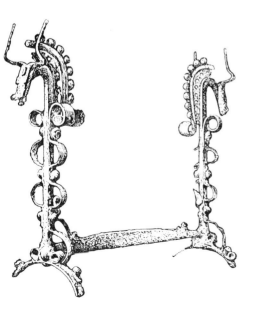

From time to time, people, often farmers ploughing their fields, unearth treasures of the Bronze and Iron Ages. Sometimes the discoveries have not been reported and are kept by the finder or merely dismissed as 'old junk' and thrown away. But the majority of the finds are exhibited in museums and include harness fittings, hilts for iron weapons, brooches, iron buckets, cauldrons and tankards and gold ornaments. Some of the items are found singly, some together, and sometimes many in hoards. Some of the Bronze Age gold torcs found in Wales may have been caches of personal valuables buried for safety during a time of danger.

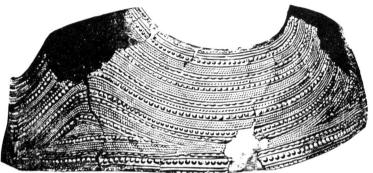

One of the most exciting finds ever made was the Mold cape which was discovered in a barrow called Bryn yr Ellyllon (see page 48). It was at one time identified as a gold peytrel (a breastplate for a pony) mounted on copper and measuring 3 feet 7 inches in length and 8 inches deep, but it is now identified as a ceremonial cape to be worn by a chief. The item is incomplete, but sufficient remains to show how it was made. It is elaborately ornamented as the illustration shows, with rows of embossed, round, oval and square nail-head elevations, separated by straight lines. Before the mound was excavated, several local people had claimed that they had seen the spectre of a man on horseback with the horse clad in golden armour.

In 1881 a bucket of bronze-bound yew wood, inscribed inside and outside with strange lettering and symbols, was found in a peat bog at Ty'r Dewin near Brynkir in Gwynedd.

In 1954 a hoard of gold torcs was found by two farmworkers at Talwrn Farm near Llanwrthwl in Powys. They were preparing a field for cultivation, and on lifting a large stone they found what at first they thought were 'old bed springs'. But when they later washed the items in soapy water they realized that they were gold. The four torcs were later declared Treasure Trove and were acquired by the National Museum of Wales in 1943.

Other gold torcs were found in 1955 in a very steep field south of Cwmjenkin farm, Heyope, Radnor. Mr Pugh, the farmer, picked up a clod of earth after ploughing a field and found three gold torcs entangled and crushed into a ball. They were disentangled at the British Museum laboratory and restored to their original condition, and are now exhibited in the National Museum of Wales.

Llyn Cerrig Bach, near Valley Airfield, Anglesey, Gwynedd SH 305766 (114)

A votive hoard was discovered in this lake in 1943 when the aerodrome was being constructed. A large number of items dating from the second century B.C. to the first century A.D. were found in the peaty edge of the lake. They included weapons, harness, chariot fittings, plaques of bronze, a shield boss and an iron slave-gang chain complete with neck shackles. In all there were 150 objects and this was the largest discovery of its kind recorded in Wales.

Llyn Fawr, south of Hirwaun, near A4061, Mid Glamorgan SS
917035 (170)

When this lake was drained in 1911 to construct a reservoir some
remarkable objects were discovered lying in the peat:

6 socketed bronze axes   2 bronze socketed sickles
2 socketed bronze chisels   1 bronze cauldron
1 bronze clasp and belt fitting 1 iron spearhead
1 crescent-shaped razor   1 wrought-iron sickle
3 bronze breast ornaments part of an iron sword

These items probably date to 500 B.C. and can now be seen in the
National Museum of Wales in Cardiff.

Caergwle Clwyd

A small shale bowl of Bronze Age date, inlaid with gold and carved to represent a ship, was found in the nineteenth century in a boggy field to the west of Caergwrle castle. There are shields hanging down the side of the boat and the waves of the sea are illustrated near the base with a zigzag inlay of gold.

Tal y Llyn, Gwynedd

A boulder beside Ystrad Gwyn (a Roman road) was once moved to reveal a hoard left by some Celts. It consisted of broken shields, chariot wheel hubs and a number of ornaments. They were all made of bronze, and perhaps at that time they were regarded as scrap metal which might later be melted down and re-used.

Moel Hebog, Gwynedd

A brass shield was found in 1784 in a bog near this hill. Its diameter was 2 feet 2 inches, its weight 4 pounds, and in the centre was a circular projection. The surface was marked with 27 smooth concentric circles.

Pentre Rhondda, Mid Glamorgan

A warrior's breastplate and helmet in very rusty condition were found in about 1830 jammed in a fissure in some crags to the west of this village. The crown of the helmet was marked with a hole, through which the wearer had probably sustained a mortal blow.

About twenty years later Jenkin Jenkins, a local man, found a rusty sword near the same rocks, but lower down the hillside. The warrior must have been thrown from the hilltop, his body caught in the fissure, and the sword flung out of his hand to fall far below into the woods where it was found.

Llyn Gwernan, near Dolgellau, Gwynedd SH 706160 (124)

A magnificent gold torque was discovered near this lake in 1823. It was 42 inches in length and 8¾ ounces in weight and dated back to the later part of the Bronze Age. A torque is a spirally twisted piece of gold that was worn around the neck as an ornament. When the Celtic tribes of Central and Western Europe were first encountered by the Romans, the torque was so generally worn by the Celts that it came to be regarded as their characteristic ornament. The gold torques taken from conquered Gauls and other Celtic opponents formed an important item of spoil, and they were bestowed as rewards and honours on the soldiers who had distinguished themselves in the campaign.

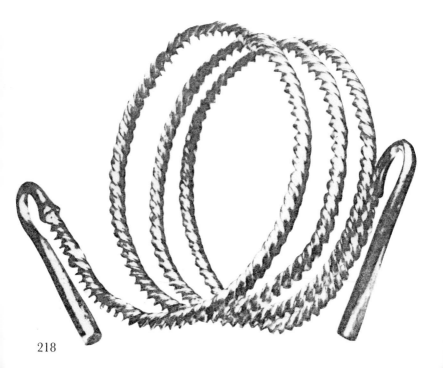

Cerrigwynion Rocks, Powys SN 970656 (147)

Some treasure was found near these rocks in 1899. James Marston of Cwmauddwr moved a big stone with an iron bar and revealed some jewellery, consisting of a gold ring, a gold necklet, a small plate of embossed gold, and a gold armlet and scroll. It has been suggested that it belonged to one of the wives of Vortigern, who was better known in Welsh history as King Gwrtheyrn (see page 114). It was probably stolen and hidden by the thief, who never managed to collect his pile of swag.

Treasures yet to be revealed

All grid references have been withheld.

Near Llanrhidian on Gower, West Glamorgan

There is supposed to be a secret chamber sealed by an iron door. If you seek it, you must take a harp with you and play a certain tune on it to open the door. Inside, there is said to be a huge heap of gold.

Llantwit Major, West Glamorgan

On the outskirts of this town a golden stag is said to be buried with its head pointing towards the west. When it is found, Llantwit Major will become important and prosperous again.

Y Garn Goch, near Ysradgynlais, Mid Glamorgan

On this hill three cauldrons full of gold are said to be awaiting discovery. There is a prediction that they will be found one day by a young girl.

Coetan Arthur, Ardudwy, Gwynedd

Treasure is supposed to be buried near this cromlech and its location is revealed when the end of a rainbow rests on the middle of the covering stone.

Castell Dinas Bran, Clwyd

A golden harp buried near the ruins of this castle is waiting to be discovered by a boy accompanied by a white dog with one silver eye:

'If you are a boy, and the owner of a white dog with a silver eye (you may not know that every such dog can see the wind), you should lose no time in going to Llangollen. Under Castell Dinas Bran there is a cave which is full of treasure. The dog will lead you to the place, and you will become rich beyond the dreams of avarice.'

W. Jenkin Thomas
The Welsh Fairy Book

Llyn Cwm Glas, Nantlle, Gwynedd

In this lake is a small island where a pile of treasure, including the golden throne of Britain, is supposed to have been hidden by Merlin to keep it safe from the Saxons.

Moel Arthur, Clwyd

Concealed on the summit of this hill fort is an iron chest with an iron ring-handle. On certain nights of the year the hiding place is supposed to be illuminated by a supernatural light. But 'whosoever digs there is always driven away by thunder, lightning, and storm'.

Hen Borth, Llanrhywydrys, north Anglesey

Two caves on the eastern side of Carmel Head are called Ogof Aur (The Golden Cave) and Ogof Arian (The Silver Cave). It is reputed that the monks from Mynachdy (Monk's House) hid their treasure in these caves, and a passage from the cellars of the original grange once led down to the secret hiding place.

Cibwr Bay, Cardigan, Dyfed

In the depths of the cave known as the Witches' Cauldron there are said to be fabulous treasures waiting to be discovered.

Twyn Tudor, Mynyddislwyn, Gwent

Somewhere inside this large mound (see page 39), near Mynyddislwyn church, is supposed to be a chest of treasure. Long ago, someone tried to dig for it but was stopped by a terrible thunderstorm that terrified the treasure hunter so much that he abandoned his search and never returned.

Llachas Moor, near Llantwit Major, West Glamorgan

A gold chain was found here in 1857 by a farm labourer: 'It was as heavy as a pound of butter, and nearly as soft, a sure sign of the purity of the gold.' In ancient times a collar or chain was known as an erwy and it was worn as a badge of distinction by warriors:

> *'A golden aerwy will be sent to some slaughter,*
> *On his goodly neck, bright and fresh.'*
> G. ap Ieuan Hen 1300 A.D.

A chain of gold worn by warrior chiefs was also known as a cadwyn. Llywarch Hen describes Cynddylan, Prince of Powys as follows:

> *'Cynddylan, eminent for sagacity of thought,*
> *Cadwynawg (wearing the chain), foremost in the hosts,*
> *The protector of Tren, whilst he lived.'*
> Elegy on Cynddylan

In another poem he referred to his own sons wearing the golden chain:

> '*Four and twenty sons I have had*
> *Wearing the golden chain, leaders of armies;*
> *Gwen was the best of them.*'

In the story of the Dream of Maxen Wledig which is contained in *The Mabinogion* there is a mention of a breichrwg, which is a golden bracelet worn by distinguished persons of both sexes, and a detailed description of a man well-decorated with golden ornaments:

'*Brechrwyau of gold were round his arms, a profusion of golden rings on his hands, a wreath of gold round his neck; and a frontlet of gold on his head, keeping up his hair and he had a magnificent appearance.*'

Llanymynach Hill, near Oswestry, Powys

A burial chamber on this hill is known as the Giant's Grave and it is said to be where a giant once buried his wife with a gold scarf tied around her neck. Over a hundred years ago three brothers broke open the tomb in search of the gold. They failed to find it and apparently all three died soon afterwards.

Bwlch y Gwyddyl (The Irishmen's Pass) near Pen y Gwryd, Gwynedd

The site of an ancient Irish settlement is to be seen at Muriaur Dre (Town Walls) near Cwm Dyli. A pile of treasure is buried here and only an Irishman will be successful in finding it.

Cwm y Bedol Arian, Gwynedd

This name translates as the 'Hollow of the Silver Slipper'. Did Cinderella pass this way?

Llyn Dinas, Nant Gwynnant, Gwynedd

Between Beddgelert and Pen y Gwryd the throne of Britain was hidden by Vortigern in a secret place covered by a stone.

Afon Caerfannel, Powys

An ancient rhyme relating to the brook called the Caerfannel, which divides the parishes of Llandetty and Llanfigan, gives the following information:

> '*On Anell's banks, within a meadow's bound,*
> *A carn, a corpse and a dagger may be found,*
> *But what's more rare, though where, not revealed,*
> *A golden cauldron and a sword concealed.*'

Treasure Trove

Under this law the Crown becomes the owner of any gold or silver that has been hidden in the soil or a building and of which the owner cannot be traced.

If the items are found on the surface then they are deemed not to be hidden and are not regarded as treasure trove, but may belong to the landowner.

Any object found in a grave or presumably thrown into a sacred lake 'as an offering to the gods' may be regarded as the property of the landowner.

If the owner had parted with the property in such a manner as to abandon it altogether, the first finder is entitled to the property. If the property was hidden in any house, or in the earth, or other private place, the owner being unknown, then the property belongs to the Crown.

14.
The Historical Significance of Welsh Place Names

'Local names, whether they belong to provinces, cities, and villages, or are the designations of rivers and mountains – are never mere arbitrary sounds devoid of meaning. They may always be regarded as records of the past, inviting and rewarding a careful historical interpretation.'

Rev. Isaac Taylor, M.A., Words and Places

The Welsh language has developed from Britannic, which at one time would have been widely spoken throughout the mainland of Britain. Out of this language Welsh, Cornish and Breton were formed, and it can be said that Welsh is the oldest surviving language in Britain. The people of southern Scotland and northern England were once Welshmen (Cymry), who spoke Cymraeg – the language of Wales.

Corruption of Welsh place names

So many Welsh place names on modern maps and signposts have been so badly mutilated that they have now become nothing less than a series of enigmatical problems. This process of mutilation has, unfortunately, been going on for more than a century. In addition, many place names have been so corrupted, in usage and in translation from language to language, that Welsh history is consequently obscured. One Welsh historian in the nineteenth century was so dismayed by the problem that he observed:

'Many Welsh appellations and local names have been so long corrupted that it would be affectation to attempt to reform them.'

The following are examples of some of the ancient names of Wales that have been unhappily Latinized and Anglicized over the centuries:

Môn was transmuted to Mona and then to Anglesey
Aberconwy to Aberconvium to Conway
Abergafeni to Abergavennium to Abergavenny

Aberogwr to Ogmore
Coed-du to Coity
Gwynfa to Wenvoe
Caerau to Carew
Magwr to Magor
Tafarn Yspytty to Spite Tavern
Gwynlliwg to Gwentllwg to Wentlooge

It was customary in ancient times in Wales for people to take their names from the places where they were born or lived, for example, Pennant, and Mostyn. But in even earlier times, however, the reverse would often apply, with places being named after people whose names now provide an important link with the history of that area:

Brecon was named after Brychan
Cardigan was named after Ceredig
Merioneth was named after Meirion
Merthyr Tydfil was named after Tydfil, who was Brychan's daughter

Examples of origins and historical importance

'In Wales, Cornwall and Brittany, it is not the "Lives" of the saints that tell us most about the existence of the saints and the natural organisation of religion, but names of places.'

M. Joseph Loth, 1910

Belan (Anglesey) is an abbreviation of Llanbeulan and this church is dedicated to Beulan, the son of Paulinus.

Bodedern (Anglesey) was the dwelling place of Edern or Edeyrn, the son of Nudd the son of Beli. He was a warrior and a poet; later in life he became religious and built a church here.

Bodferin (Anglesey) was the dwelling place of Merin, a saint of the sixth century and a descendant of Seithenin.

Cadoxton (West Glamorgan) comes from Cadoc's Town. The church here is dedicated to St Cattwg the Wise, son of Gwynlliw.

Cardigan (Dyfed) is a corruption of Cerredigion, which was the original name and refers to Ceredig, the son of Cunneda Wledig, who became king of this area at the end of the fourth century.

Ceirchog (Gwynedd) means 'abounding with oats'. The soil in this area on Anglesey has always been noted for yielding large crops of oats. The English name is Oatham.

Cilgeran (Dyfed) is derived from Cil Geran. The name Geran is an abbreviation of Geraint, who was probably the son of Erbin. Before the Norman castle was built, this place was known as Din Geraint. . .Geraint's Fortress. The prefix din was changed into Cil and the name now signifies the place or retreat of Geraint.

Dingestow (Gwent) is derived from Llandingat and is associated with Dingat, one of the sons of Brychan Brycheiniog. He was a member of Cattwg's college at Llancarfan and he founded the church of Llandingat in Llandovery. The name DUNOCAT is commemorated on a sixth-century inscribed stone which used to stand in Glen Usk Park, Powys. It is quite possibly a memorial stone to St Dingat.

Leckwith (South Glamorgan) was a name introduced by the Normans when they settled here in the eleventh century. It is a corruption of Llechwedd, meaning the steep of a hill or a hillside.

Llanabo (Anglesey) is named after Pabo Post Prydain, a noble warrior who became religious later in life and founded the church of St Llanabo. Here can be seen a stone which bears his image and the inscription – HIC JACET PABO POST PRUD CORPOS TE PRIMA.

Llanbadarn (Dyfed) was founded by Padarn who came to Wales from Brittany in 516 A.D. He attended Illtud's college (in Llantwit Major, Glamorgan) and then went north to establish his monastery here, where he gathered together 120 followers. The neighbouring town of Aberystwyth was originally known as Llanbadarn Gaerog.

Llanberis (Gwynedd) is where St Peris, the son of Helig ap Glannog, once lived.

Llanddyfnan (Gwynedd) is dedicated to Dyfnan, son of Brychan Brycheiniog

Llandegai (Gwynedd) is named after Tegai, a son of Ithael Hael. He was a sixth-century saint who founded a church here.

Llandegfed (Gwent) is where St Tegfedd (or Tegwedd) founded a church in the fifth century. She was the mother of Teilo, who became Bishop of Llandaff. Tegfedd was the daughter of Tegid Foel of Penllyn, who was drowned in Llyn Tegid (Bala Lake).

The little church at Llandegfedd is built on the spot where she was murdered by the Saxons, and it was once known as Merthyr Tegfedd (The Martyr Tegfedd).

Llandogo (Gwent) is named after Docheu, the son of Budic of Armorica (Brittany), whose memorial stone can be seen at Margam (see page 98). Docheu or Oudoceus was the third Bishop of Llandaff. Budic has his name preserved in a wood in the Wye Valley called Coed Buddig.

Llandough (South Glamorgan) is named after St Dochau (or Cyngar) who was the son of Geraint ap Lludd. His brother was Selyf, who was the father of St Cybi. It is said that Dochau was a cousin of St Illtud and Arthur.

Llandwrog (Gwynedd) is named after Twrog, who is said to have been a son of Ithael Hael of Llydaw. Twrog is also remembered in the name of Maentwrog (near Ffestiniog) and he is probably buried at Bedd Twrog on the north side of Mynydd Cilgwyn, near Carmel.

Llandybie (Dyfed) is the location where Tybie, one of the many daughters of Brychan, was murdered and a church was subsequently built in her memory.

Llandyssilio (Anglesey) was founded by Tyssilio, one of the sons of Brochwel Ysgythrog, Prince of Powys and cousin to St Asaf.

Llandysul (Dyfed) provides a memory of Tysul, a descendant of Cunedda Wledig

Llanedeyrn (South Glamorgan) is associated with Edeyrn, the son of Vortigern, who, according to Nennius, was a member of the college of St Cattwg at Llancarfan. Edeyrn established his own religious community at this site near St Mellons.

Llaneinydd (South Glamorgan) is now known as St Nicholas, but this village was originally named after Einydd, who was the son of Ithel, King of Glamorgan, the son of Arthwyr (Arthur), according to the *Liber Landavensis*. Ithel was thrown from his horse while riding across the land of Guowf, which is now called Wenvoe.

Llaneurgain (Clwyd) is the Welsh name of Northop and it recalls Eurgain, the daughter of Maelgwyn Gwynedd. She became the wife of Elidyr Mwynfawr.

Llanfaches (Gwent) recalls St Maches, the daughter of Gwynlliw (father of Cattwg), who was murdered here. The church used to be known as Merthyr Maches (Martyrdom of Maches).

Llanfaelog (Gwynedd) was founded by Maelog, the son of Caw Cawlwyd and a brother of Gildas (see page 79). Nearby is a small pool called Llyn Maelog – Maelog's Pool.

Llanfaethlu (Gwynedd) is associated with Maethlu, the son of Caradog Freichfras.

Llanfairpwllgwyngyllgogerychwyrndrobwllllandysiliogogogoch (Gwynedd) is certainly the longest name in Wales and is one of the most famous although few people can say it, let alone remember it. The usual translation is – 'St Mary's church in the hollow of the white hazel, near a rapid whirlpool and the church of St Tysilio near the red cave'. This jumble of ten words written as one is a nineteenth-century invention by a tailor from Menai Bridge. It has become a tourist attraction that has enabled the local railway station to sell the longest platform ticket in the world!

Llangadwaladr (Anglesey) takes its name from the last British prince who bore the title of King of Britain. He was Cadwaladr, the son of Cadwallon the son of Cadfan. (See page 100)

Llangaffo (Anglesey) is where Caffo, one of St Cybi's followers, was murdered by some shepherds in 545 A.D. They were incensed at the reputation bestowed on their king (Maelgwyn) by Caffo's brother Gildas.

Llangan (Dyfed) is dedicated to Cana, the daughter of Tewdr Mawr, and wife of Sadwrn (the brother of Illtud) whose name is commemorated at Llansadwrn (Dyfed).

Llangollen (Clwyd) owes its name to Collen, who founded a church here in the sixth century. He was descended from Caradog Freichfras, who drove the Irish out of Brycheiniog. Collen is believed to be buried beneath the floor of the church.

Llangrannog (Dyfed) is attributed to St Crannog the son of Carwn, the son of Ceredig.

Llansadwrn (Dyfed) church is dedicated to Sadwrn, the brother of Illtud.

Llanwnog (Powys) In this church near Newtown is a stained-glass window depicting Gwynnog, its founder, who was a son of Gildas.

Llavernock (South Glamorgan) is an example of a Norman corruption of a name. It should be Llanwenog, which means a church in a meadow.

Lleyn (Gwynedd) is an area believed to be named after Lleyn, the son of Baram. He conquered this part of the territory of the King of Gwynedd and called it the country of Lleyn.

Llyn Tegid (Gwynedd), more popularly known as Lake Bala, is named after Tegid, who was the son of Baram. According to Iolo Morgannwg, Tegid 'enacted excellent regulations for literature; restored ancient learning, which had nearly become lost, and instituted a council of bards and Druids, as of old. He continued at war with his enemies but they took him at last, through treachery, and drowned him in the great lake called from that circumstance Llyn Tegid (Tegid's Lake) in Gwynedd.'

Machen (Gwent) is named after St Meugan, the son of Gwyndaf Hen. Meugan was a member of the college of Illtyd at Llantwit Major and he died on Ynys Enlli (Bardsey Island) in 605 A.D.

Manmoel (Gwent) According to the Charters of Llancarfan, Cattwg built a church here for Macmoil, his disciple, and secured it with a rampart and erected an altar inside.

Margam (West Glamorgan) is named after Morgan Mwynfawr (Morgan the Courteous, the son of Arthwyr). For centuries this place was known as Morgan and it gradually became altered to Margam.

Merthyr Cynog (Powys) is where Cynog, the eldest son of Brychan Brycheiniog, was murdered by Saxon pagans on a hill called Y Fan, where the church was built over his grave.

Merthyr Tydfil (Mid Glamorgan) takes its name from Tydfil, another of Brychan's many daughters. She was murdered near here in about 420 A.D. The parish church is dedicated to her and is said to be built on the scene of the murder.

Penrice (West Glamorgan) is derived from Pen Rhys (Rhys's Head). He was the son of Caradoc ap Iestyn and he was beheaded here by the Normans in 1099 A.D.

Porthkerry (South Glamorgan) means the Harbour of Ceri, who was the son of Caid. He was a wise ruler who built a harbour here and constructed a fleet of ships.

Pwllheli (Gwynedd) is derived from Heli, the son of Glanog.

Pwllmeyric (Gwent) means Meurig's Pool and is derived from Pwll Meurig. It is associated with Meurig ap Tewdrig who was the father of Arthwyr (Arthur). (See page 139)

Rhossili (West Glamorgan). A church was founded here in the sixth century by St Fili, the son of Cenydd. He also gave his name to an early fort at Caer Fili (Mid Glamorgan) which in due course became Caerphilli.

St Athan (Mid Glamorgan) is derived from St Tathan, the son of Amwn Ddu, who retired here in a simple cell in the sixth century. According to the Welsh Chronicles, his remains are interred here.

Tondu (South Glamorgan) is derived from the name of a grandson of Morgan Hen and a summer house he had here called Ton (grassy plot of land) Ithael Du. He was called Ithael Ddu (Ithael the Dark) because of his black hair and beard.

Tregaron (Dyfed) was named after Caron who was King Crair and known by the Romans as Carausius. He lived in the third century and fought against the armies of Rome. It is said that when he died he was buried in the mound on which this church now stands. His memorial stone may be the inscribed stone at Penmachno (see page 111) which bears the name Caurusius.

Ystradgynlais (Mid Glamorgan) The church here is dedicated to St Gunleus (Gunleus ap Glewisseg), otherwise known as Gwynlliw. He married Gwladys, one of the daughters of Brychan, and their most famous son was Cattwg (see page 132). It has been suggested that Gunleus received this valley as a wedding gift from Brychan.

Ystrad Meurig (Dyfed) is where Meurig, the son of Meirchion, was killed and the church here is dedicated to him. He was a brave king who fought hard against the Irish Picts, but he was subsequently killed by an Irishman hiding in a wood.

Battle Sites

Amlwch (Anglesey). Several names in this area suggest that some bloody battles were waged here in ancient times.

Cadfa: 'Battleplace'

Cerrig y Llefau: 'Stones of weeping'

Rhyd y Galonastra: 'The Ford of Massacre'

Battle (Powys) near Brecon takes its name from a battle fought here in 1093 in which Bleddyn ap Maenyrch, the last of the Brychan princes was killed by Bernard de Newmarch. In this vicinity is Cwm Gwyr y Gad – 'Vale of the battle men'.

Bwlch y Gwyddel (Gwynedd) This name translates as 'The Pass of the Irishmen' and it is near Snowdon. According to tradition, it was once the scene of a battle between the Britons and the invading Irish. It would seem that the Irish won the day and settled in Nant Gwynant.

Cefn Digall (Powys) A great battle took place here on Hir Mynydd in the seventh century between Cadwallawn and Edwin, King of Northumbria. There is a circular encampment on the summit of the hill called the Brecon Ring which was probably involved in the conflict. It was said that after this great battle the Severn was coloured with blood from its source to its estuary.

Cerrig y Gwyddyl (Gwynedd) on Anglesey was the site of a great battle where Cadwallon Lawhir (The Long-handed) defeated the Irish and drove them out of North Wales (see page 162).

Devauden (Gwent) is derived from Ffawgdden, meaning beech tree. A battle took place here in 743 A.D. when the Welsh were slaughtered by the Saxon kings Ethelbald of Mercia and Cuthred of Wessex.

Gadlys (Mid Glamorgan) means 'Battle Court' and the name is linked with a battle fought in the upper part of the Aberdare valley between Rhys ap Tewdwr and Iestyn ap Gwrgan. It would seem that Iestyn's army encamped in Lower Gadlys and Rhys's army gathered in the Upper Gadlys.

Garth Maelwg (Mid Glamorgan) is the location of a battle that took place in 720 A.D. between Arfael and the Saxons. Three huge cairns are supposed to mark the burial place of those who fell. Rhiw Saeson (Saxons' Slope) is possibly the site of the battle. Arthfael was killed fighting the Saxons near Cardiff and he was buried at Roath.

Hirwaun (Mid Glamorgan) is derived from Hirwaun Wrgan, which means Gwrgan's Long Meadow. It was an area of land given to the people of Glamorgan in the ninth century as common grazing ground by Gwrgan, prince of Morgannwg. It was here, at the end of the eleventh century, that a battle was fought between Iestyyn ap Gwrgan, with his Norman allies, against the forces of Rhys ap Tewdwr, Prince of Dynevor. Rhys fled from the field and was captured and beheaded at Penrhys in the Rhondda Valley, where a monastery was later built over his burial site. There are several cairns in the Hirwaun area that are reputed to be monuments to this great battle and some explicit names in the vicinity refer to this event, for example, Maes y Gwaed (The Field of Blood), Carn y Frwydr (Battle Cairn) and Gadlys (The Hall of Battle).

Llantilio Crossenny (Gwent) According to the Book of Llandaff, this is where the Welsh King Iddon (son of Ynyr Gwent) fought the Saxons in the late sixth century. The battle was not going in Iddon's favour, so he sent for St Teilo to pray for victory. The saint stood on a mound (where the church now stands) overlooking the battle ground, and it would seem that his prayers were answered, for Iddon's men won the day. A cross was subsequently set up in Maes y Groes (Field of the Cross) to mark the spot where Teilo prayed for victory.

Llechryd (Dyfed) is the scene of a battle in 1067 between Rhys ap Tewdwr and the three sons of Bleddyn ap Cynfyn, in which the sons of Bleddyn were defeated and two of them slain on the field.

Maes Mawr y Gad (Gwynedd) on Anglesey is believed to be where the Druids were massacred by the Romans in the first century A.D. The name means 'Field of the Great Army.'

In 58 A.D., Suetonius Paulinus became Governor of Britain and decided that a mortal blow against Mona (Anglesey), where the Druids were centred, would have a devastating effect on the morale of the population in that area. He also wished to secure the pearl fisheries on the River Conwy. (Pliny recorded that Julius Caesar placed in the temple of Venus at Rome a breastplate covered with British pearls. They probably came from the River Conwy.)

Suetonius arrived in North Wales in 60 A.D. and constructed some flat-bottomed boats to carry his legionaries across the shallow waters of the Menai Straits. His cavalry crossed on the backs of their horses. The site of the crossing was probably somewhere between Aber and Beaumaris.

The Druids, with their long beards and long robes complete with white hoods, must have formed a majestic and impressive gathering, solemnly chanting their frenzied prayers and uttering curses on the Roman invaders. The very sight of the Druids struck terror into the hearts of the Roman soldiers, but they were soon coaxed into action by their general. The soldiers surged forward and descended on the Druids in overwhelming numbers – men, women and children were all slaughtered, for they deliberately exposed themselves to the enemy blows. The sacred groves were felled and burned, and the island of Mona – the sanctuary of the Druids and the seat of the Arch Druid – was left ruined and desolate.

Before long the Romans established a permanent camp and garrison at Caergybi (a post-Roman name for Holyhead). Here the churchyard walls were once part of the Roman fort (see page 162). Suetonius Paulinus was soon forced to leave the island and return to his base, for Queen Boadicea was threatening his line of communication. His name is remembered by a hill near St Asaph, called Bryn Paulin, and it is possible that he camped there one night while riding south.

The English name of Anglesey was given to the island after the battle of Llanfaes, in which Egbert was victorious over Merddyn. The Saxon king subdued Mona and in 818 A.D. renamed it Anglesey – The Isle of the Angles or English ('ey', the last syllable, is Norse for island).

Mynydd y Gaer (Mid Glamorgan), above Cwm Ogwr Fach, is a fascinating hill where numerous encampments and burial mounds can be seen. There are legends of ancient battles taking place on these heights and a mound on which a trig' point now stands is known as Mynwent y Milwyr (The Soldiers' Burial Place).

Mynydd Llangattock (Powys) Two huge cairns mark the location of a great battle which was fought here in 728 A.D. between Ethelbald the Mercian and the men of Morgannwg, led by Rhoderic Molwynog. The remains of a warrior were discovered in one of the cairns in the nineteenth century.

The waters of the Usk proved fatal to the course of Ethelbald, for, while many of the Mercians were trying to make their escape through the flooded river, they were swept away and drowned. This battle is often confused with the battle of Carno, for it took place on a location known as Mynydd y Cyrn, but the real battle of Carno was fought on the hills of Carno between Carno and Tref Eglwys in Mid Wales.

Twyn y Beddau (Powys) A large mound can be seen about two miles from Hay-on-Wye under the shadow of the Black Mountains. It is said to mark the spot where a great battle was once fought: 'The carnage was so great that the neighbouring stream, the Dulas, ran red with blood for three days afterwards.'

Suggested Books for Further Reading

Barber, Chris *Mysterious Wales* (David and Charles, Newton Abbot, 1982, Paladin paperback 1983)

Barber, Chris *Ghosts of Wales* (John Jones, Cardiff, 1979).

Bord, Janet and Colin *Mysterious Britain* (Garnstone Press 1972, Paladin paperback 1974)

Bord, Janet and Colin *The Secret Country* (Elek Books, London, 1976, Paladin paperback 1978)

Bowen, E G *The Settlements of the Celtic Saints in Wales* (University of Wales Press, Cardiff, 1956)

Giraldus, Cambrensis *Itinerary of Wales*, 1188 (J. M. Dent and Sons, London, 1908).

Chadwick, N K *The Age of Saints in the Early Celtic Church* (Oxford University Press 1961)

Evans, J G and J Rhys *The Book of Llan Dav* (Liber Landavensis) (Oxford, 1983)

Fenton, Richard *A Historical Tour through Pembrokeshire 1811.*

Giraldus, Cambrensis *Itinerary of Wales*, 1188.

Grimes, W F *The Prehistory of Wales* (National Museum of Wales, Cardiff, 1951)

Grimes, W F *The Megalithic Monuments of Wales* (National Museum of Wales, Cardiff, 1936)

Grinsell, L V *Folklore of Prehistoric Sites in Britain* (David and Charles, Newton Abbot, 1976)

Hall, S C and A M *The Book of South Wales, the Wye and the Coast 1861* (reprinted by Charlotte James, England 1980)

Hawkes, Jacquetta *A Guide to the Prehistoric and Roman Monuments in England and Wales* (Chatto and Windus, London, 1951)

Jones, Francis *The Holy Wells of Wales* (University of Wales Press, Cardiff, 1954)

Jones, Gwyn T *Welsh Folklore and Custom* (republished by D. S. Brewer, Cambridge, 1979)

Jones, Gwyn T and Jones, Thomas *The Mabinogion* (Everyman's Library, London, 1974)

Laing, Lloyd *Celtic Britain* (Routledge and Kegan Paul, London, 1979, Paladin paperback 1981)

Leland, John *Itinerary* (Centaur Press, Arundel, 1964)

Lewis, Samuel *Topographical Dictionary of Wales* 1833

Monmouth, Geoffrey of *History of the Kings of Britain* (Penguin, London, 1966)

Nash, Williams V E *The Early Christian Monuments of Wales* (University of Wales, Cardiff, 1950)

North, F J *Sunken Cities, Some Legends of the Coasts and Lakes of Wales* (University of Wales Press, Cardiff, 1957)

Owen, Trefor *Welsh Folk Customs* (1959)

Folklore, Myths and Legends of Britain (Reader's Digest and Hodder and Stoughton, London, 1973)

Rees, W J *Lives of the Cambro British Saints* (Abergavenny 1853)

Sikes, Wirt *British Goblins, 1880* (E P Publishing, Wakefield, 1973)

Trevelyan, Marie *Folklore and Folk Stories of Wales* (Elliot Stock, London, 1909)

Underwood, Guy *The Pattern of the Past* (Sphere Books, London, 1972)

Wade, Evans, A W *Welsh Christian Origins* (Aldus Press, Oxford, 1934)

Watkins, Alfred *The Old Straight Track* (Methuen and Co., London, 1925, Garnstone Press, 1975)

Index

(Note: Figures in bold type refer to illustrations)